C000216419

ALDGATE AND STEPNEY TRAMWAYS

Robert J Harley

I dedicate this book to my mother, Margaret, who spent her childhood years in the 1930s at a house overlooking the Pier Head, St.Katherine's Dock. I hope many of the views of Aldgate, Gardiner's Corner and the surrounding area will rekindle lost memories.

Cover Picture: A February day in 1939 is frozen in time as trams congregate at Aldgate terminus. Car 1111 has barely a week left of active service before the introduction of trolleybuses on replacement route 653. (W.A.Camwell)

Cover Colours: These reflect the livery worn by LCC tramcars in the 1920s.

First published February 1996

ISBN 1 873793 70 7

Design - Deborah Goodridge

Published by Middleton Press
Easebourne Lane
Midhurst
West Sussex
GU29 9AZ
Tel: 01730 813169
Fax: 01730 812601

Printed & bound by Biddles Ltd,
Guildford and Kings Lynn

CONTENTS

INTRODUCTION AND ACKNOWLEDGEMENTS

Tramways once played a vital role in the communities of the East End of London; for many of the poorest citizens of the capital the trams offered the only alternative to walking. The electric cars were frequent and reliable, they turned up in all weathers and they provided a social service based on cheap fares. In short, the trams were always there when you needed them.

This volume completes a quartet of books written to celebrate the tramways of East London. Other works published by Middleton Press are: Ilford and Barking Tramways, East Ham and West Ham Tramways, Walthamstow and Leyton Tramways. My gratitude goes to all those photographers, past and present, who have made our pictorial journey possible. The roll of honour reads thus: W.A.Camwell, C.Carter, D.W.K.Jones, C.F.Klapper, E.G.P. Masterman, H.B.Priestley, G.N.Southerden, D.A.Thompson and H.Wightman. I must also thank Mrs S. Leitch for permission to use views taken by her late father, Dr H. Nicol. Collections of photographs made available by Dave Jones, John Meredith and John Price have greatly enhanced the range of this book. Extra information for the rolling stock section has been supplied by John Wills; Terry Russell has again provided one of his splendid car drawings. Thanks also to G.Croughton for supplying tickets used.

A special word of thanks is due to B.J.Cross who has generously allowed some of his extensive postcard collection to be used; many of his rare views document horse tramway operation in the East End.

Traffic notices and other London Transport publications are reproduced by permission of London Transport Museum.

GEOGRAPHICAL SETTING

The East End of London is bounded to the west by the City. The River Lea was once the eastern frontier between the London County Council and the local authorities of Metropolitan Essex. The establishment of the Greater London Council in 1965 resulted in the setting up of an enlarged Borough of Hackney. Bethnal Green, Poplar and Stepney were amalgamated into the new Borough of Tower Hamlets.

All maps are to the scale of 25" to the mile (1:2500) unless otherwise stated. Specialist tramway track maps drawn by the late Frank Merton Atkins have also been used to augment the text.

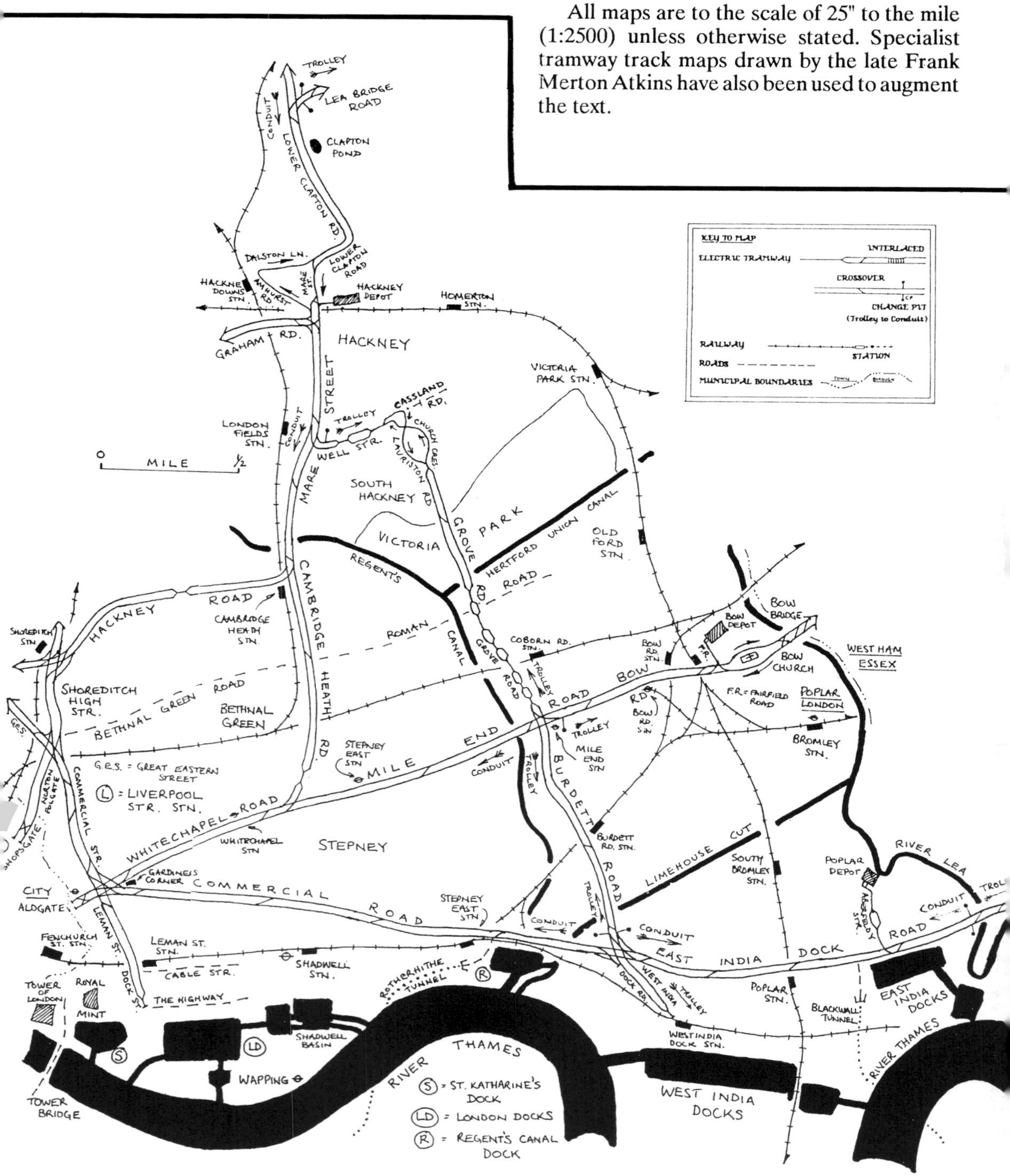

HISTORICAL BACKGROUND

Human settlements on the north bank of the Thames date back many centuries. The arrival of railways in 1839/40 accelerated urban growth in the corridors connecting the eastern suburbs of London with the City. Soon it became apparent that horse omnibuses could not handle all the short distance public transport needs of the local populus and a start was made late in 1869 to construct a system of horse tramways which were to serve the main traffic arteries of the East End. The section between Whitechapel Church and Bow Bridge opened on 9th May 1870. Aldgate was reached on 1st March 1871 and by the end of the decade a network of lines conveyed passengers from Poplar, Stratford and Clapton to the terminus on the City boundary at Aldgate. Unfortunately no tramways were ever allowed to cross the City of London, thereby denying the North Metropolitan Tramways Co. useful access to the centres of business and commerce. In the 1890s the company reached its peak with a fleet of horse cars which were painted different colours according to route allocation. The following local services were operated:

Poplar to Bloomsbury..	brown cars
Poplar to Aldgate..	yellow cars
Stamford Hill to London Docks..	yellow cars
Hackney to Aldgate..	red cars
Hackney to Aldersgate..	green cars
Lower Clapton to Bloomsbury..	blue cars/yellow cars
Leytonstone, Stratford to Aldgate..	blue cars
West India Dock to South Hackney..	yellow cars

The heyday of equine power was short lived and the advance of new technology gave an impetus to local authorities to acquire the North Metropolitan lines and rebuild them for

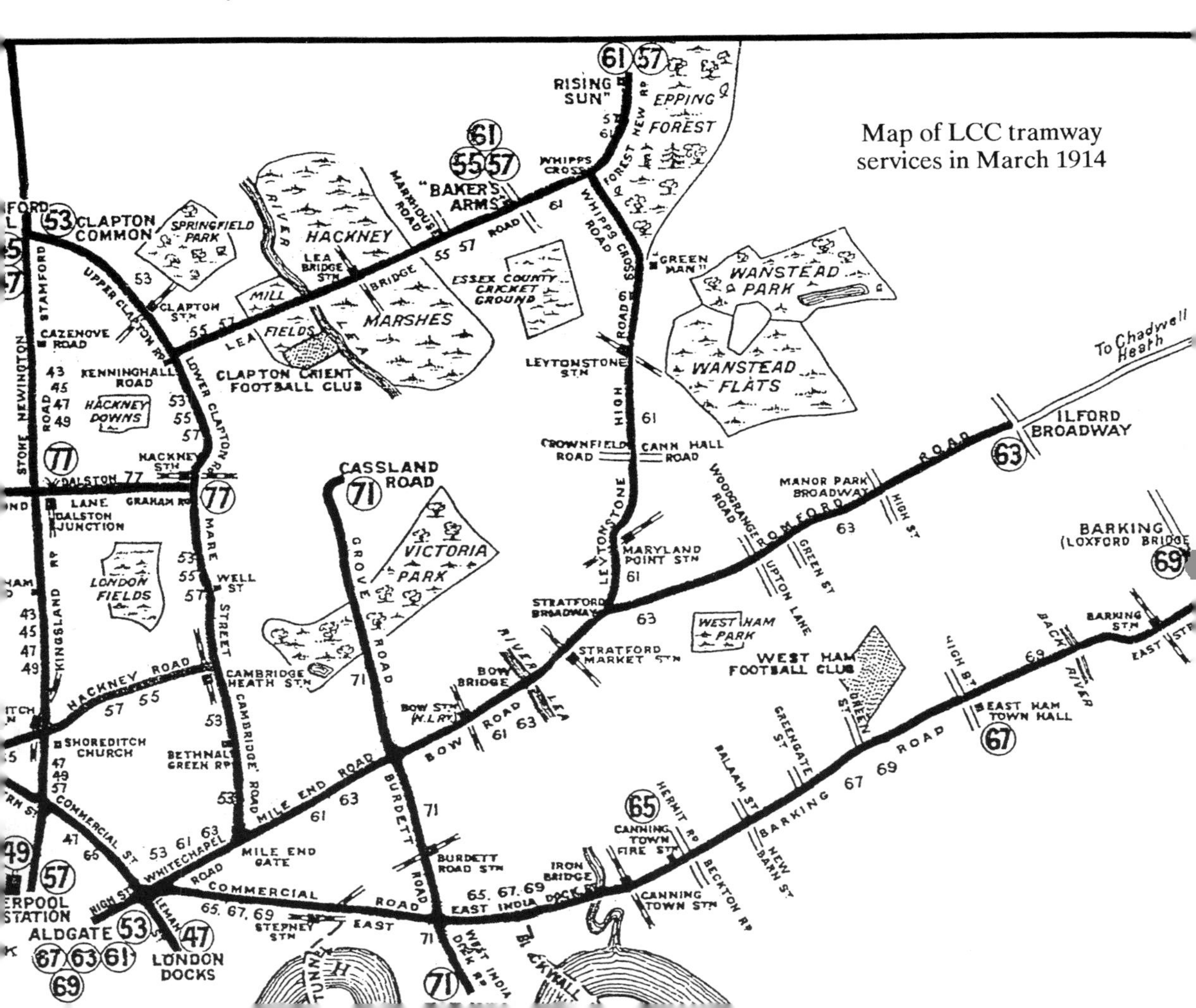

Map of LCC tramway services in March 1914

electric operation. The London County Council settled on an expensive underground conduit system to supply power to its tramcars. However, local authorities east of the River Lea adopted the tried and tested overhead wire method which was far cheaper than the conduit. On 15th December 1906 electric cars first linked Aldgate with Poplar, and by 1913 all local routes, with exception of the West India Dock to South Hackney section, had been converted. Not only were the familiar LCC cars seen at Aldgate, but also vehicles belonging to other municipal operators such as East Ham, West Ham, Leyton and Barking began to appear on through services to the Essex suburbs. Change pits which handled the transition from overhead to conduit were installed at Iron Bridge, Poplar and at the eastern end of Mile End Road.

Attempts had been going on for many years to penetrate the City of London. Sadly, the LCC was always thwarted and only one minor victory was achieved in 1913 when tracks were laid from Norton Folgate to a terminus in Bishopsgate opposite Liverpool Street Station.

In March 1914 the following local services were operated by the LCC:

43 Stamford Hill to Holborn
45 Stamford Hill to Moorgate
47 Stamford Hill to London Docks
49 Stamford Hill to Liverpool Street Station
53 Clapton Common to Aldgate
55 Leyton to Bloomsbury (joint with Leyton)
57 Leyton to Liverpool Street Station (joint with Leyton)
61 Leyton to Aldgate (joint with Leyton and West Ham)
63 Ilford Broadway to Aldgate (joint with East Ham and West Ham)
65 Canning Town Fire Station to Bloomsbury
67 East Ham Town Hall to Aldgate (joint with East Ham and West Ham)
69 Barking, Loxford Bridge to Aldgate (joint with Barking, East Ham and West Ham)
71 Victoria Park to West India Docks (horse car service)
77 Hackney to Dalston Junction

All night services

Stamford Hill to Holborn
Bow to Aldgate
Poplar to Bloomsbury

At the outbreak of the First World War in August 1914, the Victoria Park line had still to be electrified. Horse cars working this section disappeared overnight shortly after the declaration of war - the army simply moved in and requisitioned the motive power! Long suffering local citizens had to wait a few years more for the return of their tramway and the conversion to overhead trolley operation was finally effected in December 1921. An extension of track in Well Street included a new change pit on a connection to existing conduit lines in Mare Street. Service 77 replaced former horse car service 71 and it now ran from West India Docks to Aldersgate.

Improvements to rolling stock followed throughout the 1920s and early 1930s, but the imposition of the London Passenger Transport Board in 1933 put an end to tramway expansion in the capital.

Local tram services as operated by London Transport:

31 Wandsworth High Street to Hackney (Clarence Road)
43 Stamford Hill to Holborn
47 Stamford Hill to London Docks
49 Edmonton Town Hall to Liverpool Street Station
53 Tottenham Court Road to Aldgate
55 Leyton Station (LNER) to Bloomsbury
57 Chingford Mount to Liverpool Street Station
61 Leyton (Bakers Arms) to Aldgate
63 Ilford Broadway to Aldgate
65 Poplar (Blackwall Tunnel) to Bloomsbury
67 Barking Broadway to Aldgate
71 Aldersgate to Aldgate
77 West India Docks to Aldersgate
81 Woodford (Napier Arms) to Bloomsbury

All night trams

Stamford Hill to Holborn
Poplar (Blackwall Tunnel) to Bloomsbury

Plans were soon drawn up for the total conversion of the system to trolleybus operation. In the late 1930s new overhead wires for the replacing vehicles began to appear throughout the area and the trams began to disappear. Finally on 9th June 1940 services 65 and 67 fell to the trolleybus and the sound of tramcars passing Gardiner's Corner faded for good.

Years of opening

	Horse	Electric
Whitechapel to Stratford	1870	1909
Aldgate to Poplar	1872	1906
Shoreditch to London Docks	1888	1907
Shoreditch to Bishopsgate	1878/79	1907
Hackney Road	1873	1907
West India Docks to South Hackney	1872/79/85	1921
Lower Clapton to Whitechapel	1873	1909

ALDGATE TERMINUS

1. We begin our journey in the 1870s. Here at the junction of Mansell Street and Aldgate High Street a North Metropolitan horse car waits at the end of the track. Covers are provided for top deck passengers to use in inclement weather. Those hardy souls on the "outside" would normally consist of workmen and clerks who wanted to save money on the train or bus fare. Contemporary social conventions decreed that the lower saloon was the province of ladies, children, the elderly and infirm, and of course the occasional city gent who did not care to mix with the "hoi polloi" who were braving the elements on the top deck! (R.J.Harley Coll.)

2. On view is a variety of steam, electric, internal combustion and human traction. In the foreground where the tramlines finish is tangible evidence of the British class system at work. Whereas buses were tolerated in the City of London, tramcars were definitely infra dig. (LCC official photo)

3. Evening rush hour on 24th May 1934 sees plenty of activity at the terminus. Inspite of their being no through tram services into the City, this was a convenient point for passengers to change to the Underground at the adjacent

Aldgate East Station. The Metropolitan Railway first arrived at Aldgate in 1876, and electrification of most District and Metropolitan lines was completed by 1905. (Borough of Stepney)

4. A former West Ham car stands at the end of the track whilst traffic crosses into Middlesex Street. The name of this thoroughfare was originally Petticoat Lane until altered in July 1846. Some of the hustle and bustle of the local street markets can be glimpsed in Goulston Street next to the Underground station. (Borough of Stepney)

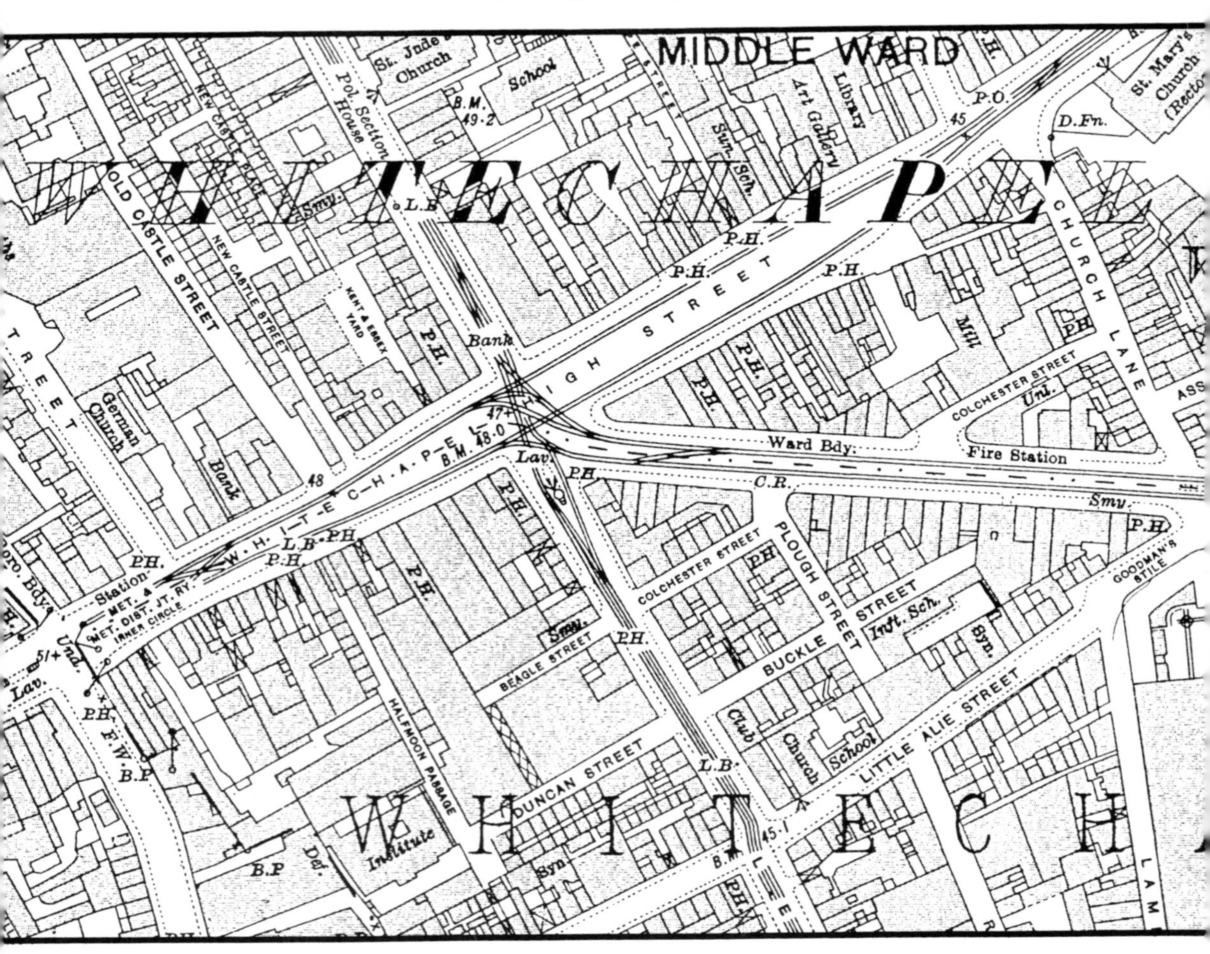

Extract from OS map, 1916 edition

5. We now descend to ground level and look east towards Gardiner's Corner. Track relaying is in full swing on this September day in 1929. This work has not hampered deliveries to a number of retail establishments. On the left of the picture the margarine boxes are lettered in both English and Hebrew. (LCC official photo)

UNDERGROUND
Cerebos
beer is best
GOLD FLAKE
NATIONAL

ARREN, SONS & Cº LTD
PRINT
CHARLES B. WOOD

6. Car 2057, a former Walthamstow vehicle, heads a line up of cars waiting to depart. New traction standards for the replacing trolley-buses have already been planted. (W.A.Camwell)

1091.—TRACK RECONSTRUCTION—ALDGATE.

Notice to Drivers.

During the reconstruction of track at Aldgate, the speed of cars over the temporary track must not exceed **5 miles an hour.**

LT circular July 1936

7. LCC car 921 is outbound to Ilford Broadway on service 63. This journey was timed at 45 minutes and the single fare was sixpence (2p). On the inbound track an East Ham car waits behind a Leyton car on service 61. (G.N.Southerden)

8. People are facing up to the first winter of the Second World War. All the trams seen here have been adapted to conform with black out regulations; headlamp masks and white painted fenders are now compulsory. The wartime emergency did not stop the trolleybus conversion of services 61 and 63 which took place on 5th November 1939. (J.H.Price Coll.)

AROUND GARDINER'S CORNER

9. The increase in motor traffic throughout the 1930s did not bring about the total eclipse of horse drawn vehicles. The Hays Wharf carter in the centre of the picture keeps a tight rein on his horse as he creeps up behind car 94. All are waiting for the policeman on point duty at Gardiner's Corner. (J.H.Meredith Coll.)

10. The photographer has managed to find a vantage point in the Gardiner and Co. building. We observe a mixture of public and private vehicles all trying to enter the City from Whitechapel High Street and Commercial Road. On the tramway scene we note that not all cars have fitted with two trolley poles and that several trams still lack drivers' windscreens. Car 1209 on service 67 is about to cross the traffic stream behind car 303. The date of this view is 16th May 1934. (Borough of Stepney)

11. Car 180 accelerates across the junction on the first leg of its journey to Leyton. Service 61 also passed the fringes of Epping Forest and the trams provided a popular means of escape for workers who wished to spent their Bank Holidays sampling the fresh air of rural Essex. These excursions are also featured in companion album *Walthamstow and Leyton Tramways*. (C.F.Klapper)

12. In the centre background the line of Commercial Street stretches into the distance. The southern section of Commercial Street from Whitechapel High Street to Christ Church, Spitalfields was opened in 1845. Horse trams appeared in November 1888 and the tracks were electrified in January 1907. In the foreground of this July 1912 scene we see a gathering of LCC eight wheelers with a solitary West Ham four wheeler passing in front of Webb's Seven Stars Inn. (B.J.Cross Coll.)

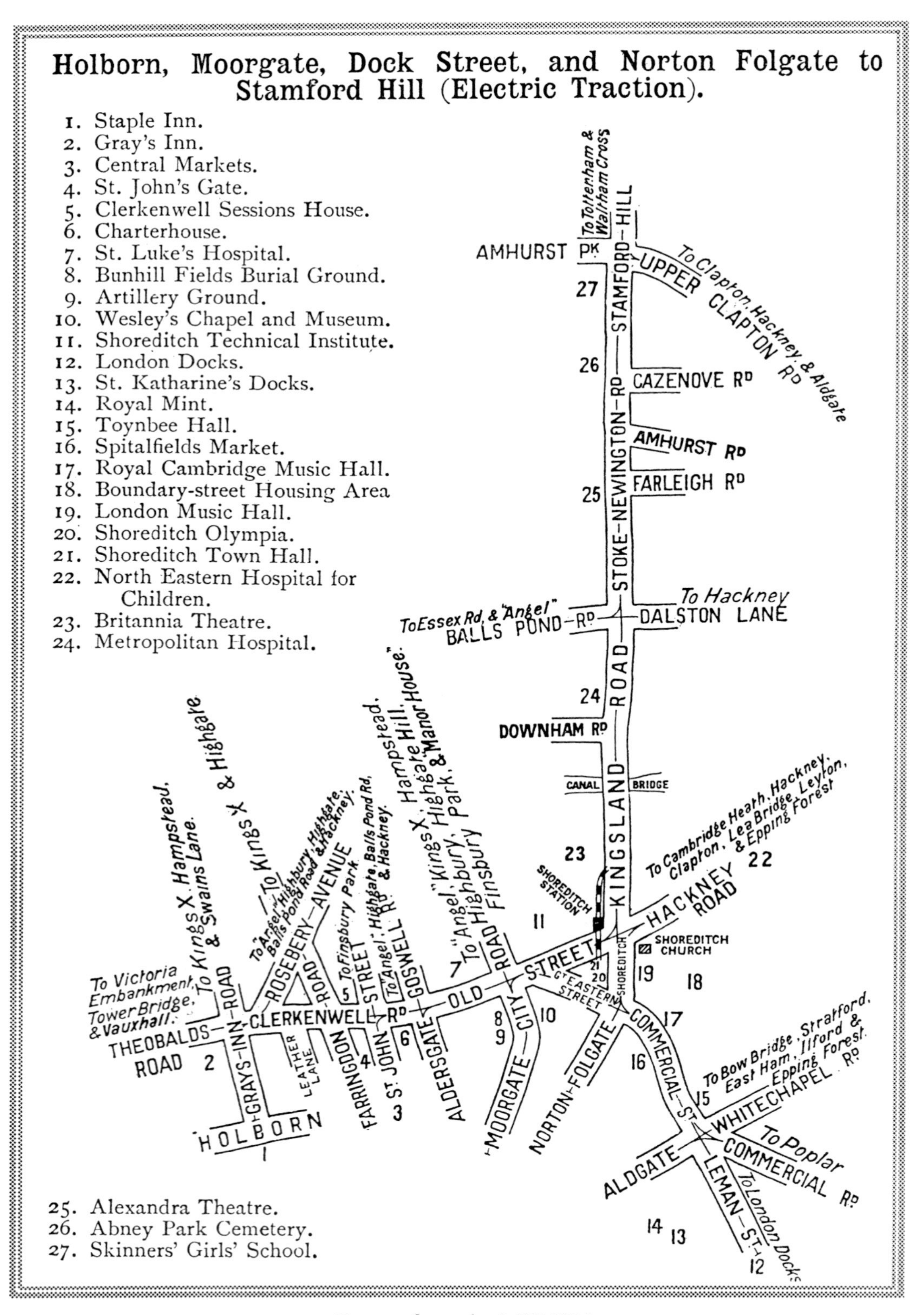

Extract from the LCC 1911 Tramways Guide.

13. The date is 10th November 1928 and a pedestrian darts in front of a packed LCC car. The tram displays the FULL board above the motorman. Service 65 was extended weekday rush hours to East Ham Town Hall from its normal terminus by Blackwall Tunnel. (H.Nicol)

14. The tracks from Leman Street into Commercial Street are traversed by car 743. The trip from London Docks to Stamford Hill was timed at 31 minutes by 47 tram. This view was taken on a rather grey Saturday afternoon in October 1928. (G.N.Southerden)

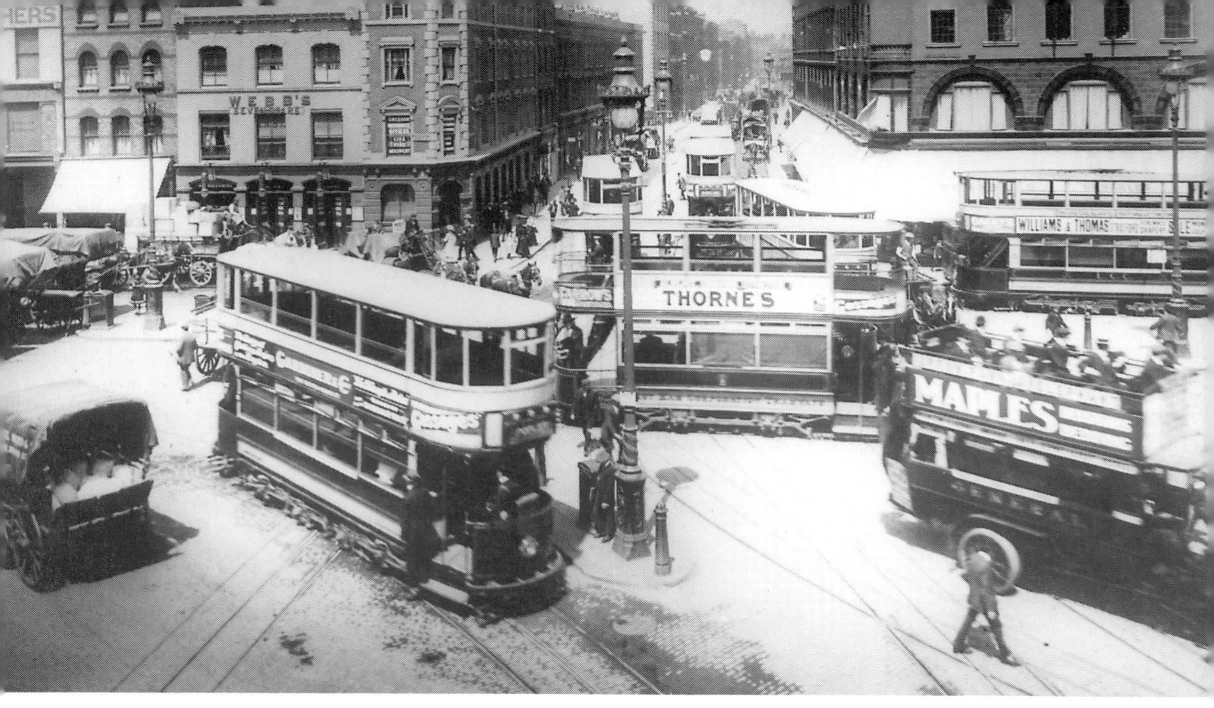

15. A week after the collapse of the dockers' strike in June 1912 and trade is getting back to normal. Buying and selling, importing and exporting, were the keys to the well being of this part of London. All roads leading to Gardiner's Corner could expect this sort of activity during working hours. (R.J.Harley Coll.)

16. This March 1909 scene depicts the transition period from horse to electric traction. An electric tram belonging to class E waits for the horse car to clear the junction before it heads off into Commercial Road. (B.J.Cross Coll.)

17. Commercial Road was constructed in 1800/02 as a direct linking route from Whitechapel to the East India Docks. The western end seen here was completed in 1870 and two years later the first horse tramway was laid between Aldgate and Poplar. East Ham car 66 has just passed a central island containing a tramways section box complete with telephone for the duty inspectors at Gardiner's Corner. (G.N.Southerden)

18. At almost exactly the same location as the previous view, an East Ham single truck car bumps over the lines which disappear behind the tram into Leman Street. The following motor bus is one of the famous NS types used by the London General Omnibus Company. Readers familiar with the traffic mad mayhem now a regular feature of this location in the 1990s, may wish to ponder whether a large roundabout and wholesale demolition has enhanced this area to any degree at all. (G.N.Southerden)

19. The whole junction and the approach tracks were renewed in 1929; the work lasted from August to October. During this period services terminated on the nearest crossover to the roadworks. Leman Street was unserved as a shuttle car would have been unable to reach a depot at night. The workmen laboured hard - hand tools and muscle power brought together the rails like a giant construction set. Each piece of track was numbered.
(LCC official photo)

20. At the end of a row of trams is this Leyton E3 class car which has been experimentally fitted with truck side plates. The 53 in front bears a poster extolling the virtues of a pleasure ride out to Highgate at a cost of just tuppence (less than 1p!). (G.N.Southerden)

21. Whitechapel High Street in the mid 1930s provides a temporary reserved track for car 89 on its way to Ilford. The advert on the car's side indicates an attempt to interest the dyed-in-the-wool British sports fan in some trans-atlantic fare to supplement his traditional diet of football, greyhounds and the speedway.
(B.J.Cross Coll.)

HOSIERY & UNDERWEAR
61
DOGS LOVE VIMS
BAKERS ARMS
ROSES VALUE
TURKISH BATHS
53
HIGHGATE
MIDDAY
2/-
DIRECT
TRANSFER
MONDAY
FRIDAY

63
ILFORD BDWY
BASEBALL WEST HAM STADIUM
DRIVE
CAUTION
SLOWLY
PLEASE BE CAREFUL
89

22. This picture is at the same spot as the previous view. It depicts the repositioning of the permanent way in August 1929. The haymarket which had traditionally occupied the centre of the highway was given its marching orders in 1927. The expulsion of the hay wains back to Constable country allowed the realignment shown here.
(LCC official photo)

23. The London Hospital was founded in 1740. A North Metropolitan horse car passes this fine building which is situated at the eastern end of Whitechapel Road not far from Sidney Street. On 2nd/3rd January 1911 trams carried onlookers fascinated by the siege and subsequent shoot out in Sidney Street between two fugitives from justice and police marksmen backed up by a detachment of the Scots Guards. The Home Secretary, Mr Winston Churchill also made an appearance. (B.J.Cross Coll.)

This extract from an LT circular of August 1938 demonstrates an attempt by the Board to make sure that staff did not sport political badges whilst on duty.

1993.—WEARING OF BADGES.

As from the 1st September, 1938, the only badge authorised to be worn, apart from that of the Board and the licence badge, is that of the Union recognized by the Board. Other symbols must not be worn by staff in uniform without consent.

24. At the foot of the appropriately named Dock Street was the London Docks terminus of service 47. Things seem to be a lot quieter in this July 1938 view than they were on 11th October 1936 when the area centred on the nearby Cable Street was the focus of a running battle between Mosley's Blackshirts, the police and various workers' groups. At the height of the riot, trams were engulfed by a sea of people and all traffic at Gardiner's Corner came to an abrupt halt. (W.A.Camwell)

LIMEHOUSE

25. This is the centre of Limehouse in the first decade of the twentieth century. To the left of the horse tram is the Passmore Edwards Sailors' Palace constructed in 1901, whilst the spire in the background belongs to the fine church of St.Anne, Limehouse, designed by Hawksmoor and begun in 1712. The church was later extensively damaged in the Blitz of 1941. (B.J.Cross Coll.)

26. Car 929 pulls up at a conveniently situated pedestrian refuge. A cheery word is passed to the conductor in anticipation of the cheap midday fares as advertised by the lower saloon window. (H.B.Priestley)

Extract from OS map, 1916 edition

27. We look along East India Dock Road just in time to catch a 77 tram crossing into Burdett Road. Note the two forms of power supply: overhead wire for the service 77 car and the more expensive conduit for the 65 tramcar waiting by the taxi rank for the signal to proceed. (H.B.Priestley)

28. A good idea of the service provided along West India Dock Road can be gauged by this photo. Cars 901 and 1147 are waiting for a sister vehicle to leave the single track terminal stub by the bridge in the background. (W.A.Camwell)

29. We move in closer to observe car 892 with another tram in the distance pictured against a skyline of warehouses and dock cranes. On the opposite side of the road there is an STL type bus on route 56 which connected the Isle of Dogs with Mile End. (H.B.Priestley)

31. A lone tram faces towards West India Dock Road. The docks themselves were built under the supervision of the engineer William Jessop and the first section opened in 1802. (D.A.Thompson)

←

30. A quiet moment at the terminus finds the conductor half hidden by the staircase. Perhaps he was indulging in a crafty cigarette? If he wanted some reading matter, he could always pick up a copy of the News of the World which was publishing an Australian account of the controversial "bodyline" cricket tour of 1933. (W.A.Camwell)

77 WEST INDIA DOCKS — ALDERSGATE
Via Burdett Rd., Mile End, Victoria Pk., Hackney, Dalston, Essex Rd., Angel, Goswell Road. Through fare 5d. Service interval, 4-8 mins. Journey time, 46 mins. Additional cars operate West India Docks—Southgate Road on Sundays, Service interval 3 mins.

	MON. to FRI. First		MON. to FRI. Last	SATURDAY First		SATURDAY Last	SUNDAY First	SUNDAY Last	
West India Docks to Aldersgate	4 52	5 18	1030	4 52	5 18	1121	8 12	1125	......
West India Docks to Angel Islington	4 52	5 18	1050	4 52	5 18	1121	8 12	1125	......
West India Docks to Hackney Station	4 52	5 18	12 7	4 52	5 18	1247	7 44	1255	......
Aldersgate to West India Docks	4 2	5 2	1119	4 2	5 2	12 0	9 2	1210	......
Aldersgate to Hackney Station	4 2	5 2	1119	4 2	5 2	12 6	9 2	1210	......
Hackney Stn. to West India Docks	4 23	4 54	1143	4 23	4 54	1222	7 21	1232	......
Hackney Stn. to Aldersgate	3 30	4 28	1052	3 30	4 28	1143	8 34	1147	......
Angel, Islington to Hackney Stn.	4 6	5 7	1131	4 6	5 7	12 9	9 5	1213	......

Extract from the December 1935
timetable for service 77

32. Trolleybus wiring has now been installed to a new turning loop as car 896 lays over at the terminus. The date is 13th August 1939 and only a few more precious days of peace remain before the coming cataclysm.
(B.J.Cross Coll.)

33. Nowadays the bridge behind the tram carries the tracks of the Docklands Light Railway, opened in 1987. Tall office buildings now dominate the quaintly named Canary Wharf and Heron Quays. All this is in the future as the conductor puts up the trolley pole under the inverted trough which acted as a guide for the trolley head. (D.Jones Coll.)

34. On the old borough boundary between Stepney and Poplar the trams have to wait patiently as the Metropolitan Police ensure that supplies are not waylaid by striking dockers. The LCC tramways also provided transport for many local councillors and politicians. One such was Clement Attlee, MP for Limehouse, who later rose to be Prime Minister in the Labour government of 1945-51. (R.J.Harley Coll.)

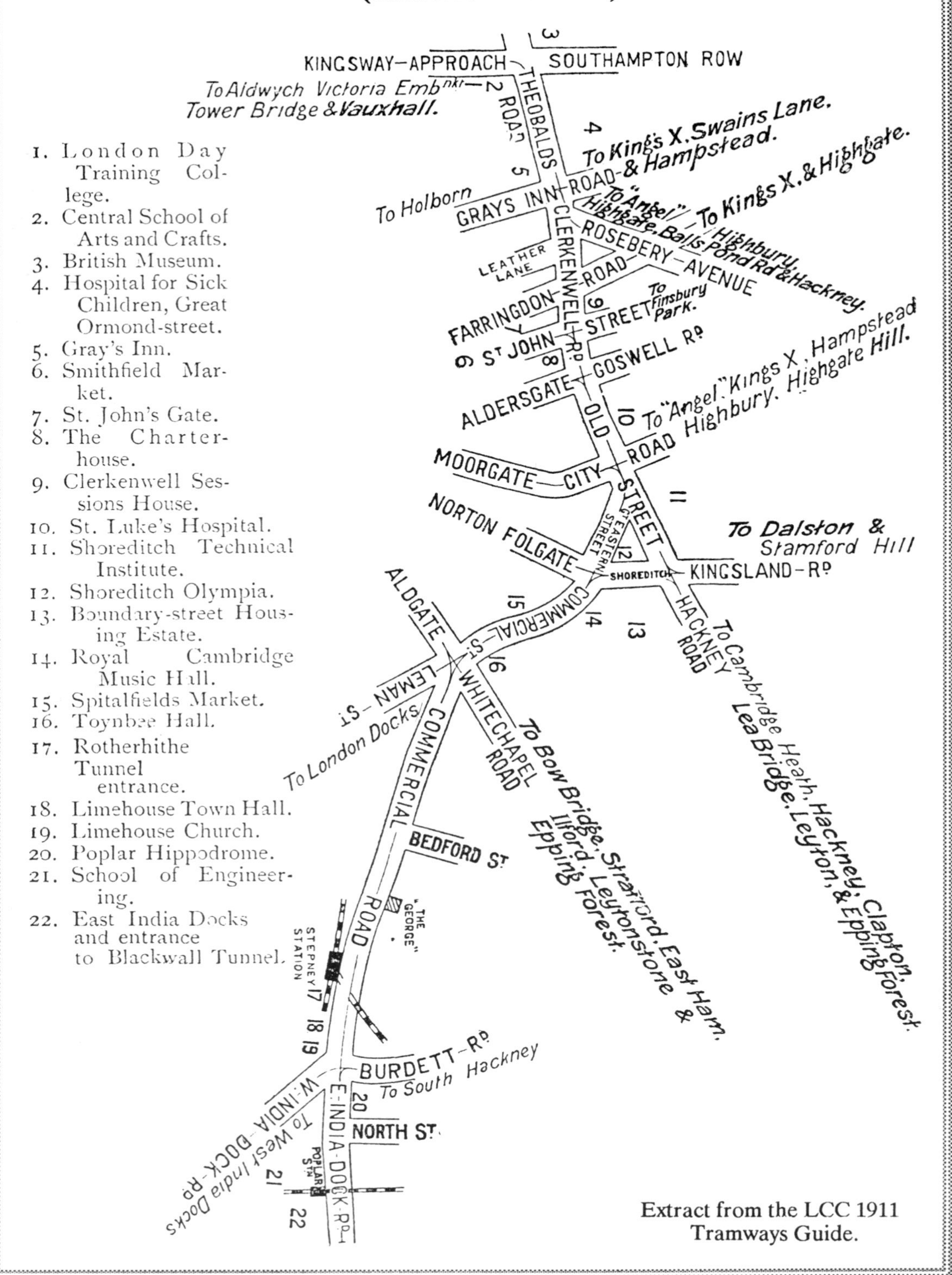

Extract from the LCC 1911 Tramways Guide.

35. The twice nightly variety performances at the Poplar Hippodrome offered a welcome break from the daily grind. Car 1285 shows ALDGATE on the front indicator and at night the three lamps above would be illuminated in a sequence of BLANK-RED-BLANK. Another aid to travellers who had difficulty reading was the introduction of side destination boards painted red to distinguish the Poplar to Bloomsbury service. In late 1912 service numbers began to replace the coloured bulbs. (B.J.Cross Coll.)

36. On the corner of Upper North Street and East India Dock Road stands William Theis's bakers shop. As we look eastwards the tram has the road pretty much to itself in this pre-First World War scene. Tragedy struck the area on 13th June 1917; 18 children perished when a stray German bomb hit the LCC school in Upper North Street. (B.J.Cross Coll.)

37. Poplar Station was built in 1852 and opened in 1866. It once served as an interchange point with the trams and buses. The station closed in 1944 after it was struck by a V1 flying bomb. It was subsequently reopened as All Saints on the Docklands Light Railway. (D.Jones Coll.)

38. The large gateway on the right of the picture leads to the East India Docks. It is flanked by transit warehouses for the import dock. The tram on service 67 passes across the northern approach road to the Blackwall Tunnel which was opened in 1897. Plans for a tramway connection under the Thames to the southern LCC system were never implemented. (R.J.Harley Coll.)

Extract from OS map, 1916 edition

39. A car waits for passengers by the Blackwall Tunnel. Aside from the usual commercial adverts, there is a poster for the famous LCC Shilling All Day ticket. This bargain facility enabled thousands of Londoners to explore their capital city. (G.N.Southerden)

40. Traffic waits either side of the junction for vehicles to emerge from the tunnel. After the trams finished in 1940, the pedestrian island and traffic light had to be repositioned so as not to interfere with the replacing trolleybuses. However, the real transformation of this area came with the upgrading of Blackwall Tunnel which began in the late 1950s. A second road tunnel completed in 1967 is now reached by an underpass and connecting dual carriageway. (H.B.Priestley)

41. Poplar Depot was constructed in two phases from 1906-11 and it had a capacity of around 90 tramcars. At the back of the building there was a wharf adjacent to the River Lea, here permanent way supplies were unloaded from barges. In 1940 work is going on to install the necessary equipment for trolleybuses; a temporary overhead to conduit change pit has been created at the entrance. The plough shift attendant is about to fork the plough under car 1252. Two spare ploughs stand propped up against the depot wall. (D.Jones Coll.)

42. Inside the building the changeover to the trolleybuses is but days away. Many of the tram maintenance pits have been filled in and all the conduit equipment has been removed, thereby necessitating car movements powered by the trolleybus overhead. The replacing vehicles lasted until 1959 when Poplar Garage then had the dubious honour of receiving a fleet of Routemaster buses. The depot closed in November 1985 and it has since been demolished. (D.Jones Coll.)

Extract from the December 1935
timetable for service 65

65 **POPLAR (Blackwall Tunnel) — BLOOMSBURY•**
Via Commercial Rd. Commercial St. Old St. Clerkenwell Road. Extended to East Ham Town Hall Weekday Rush Hours, and to Barking Broadway Saturdays p.m
Service Interval Bloomsbury—E. Ham Town Hall 2-3 mins. E. Ham, Town Hall—Barking, 4 mins. Journey time, Bloomsbury—Blackwall Tun. 32 mins.,— E. Ham Town Hall 51 mins.,—Barking Bdy. 57 mins. Through fare 6d.
• CERTAIN CARS OPERATE TO & FROM SMITHFIELD MARKET, WEEKDAY RUSH HOURS.

	MON. to FRI.			SATURDAY			SUNDAY		
	First		Last	First		Last	First		Last
Poplar (Blackwall Tunnel) to Bloomsbury..	4 26	5 5	1130	4 26	5 5	12 4	4 51	5 4	1144
Canning Town (Iron Bridge) to Bloomsbury	4 23	5 2	8 54	4 23	5 2	12 2	......	......	......
Canning Town (Fire Station) to Bloomsbury	5 56	6 2	8 52	5 56	6 2	12 0	......	......	......
East Ham Town Hall to Bloomsbury, morning	6 50	6 56	8 29	6 50	6 56	8 29	......	......	......
" " " " " afternoon	4 48	4 51	8 38	1231	1234	11 14	......	......	......
Bloomsbury to Canning Town Fire Station....	5 43	5 54	7 41	5 43	5 53	11 56	......	......	......
Bloomsbury to Poplar (Aberfeldy St.)........	5 8	5 43	12 6	5 8	5 43	12 40	5 27	5 40	1216
Bloomsbury to East Ham Town Hall, morning	6 14	6 20	7 22	5 53	5 59	7 22	......	......	......
" " " " " " afternoon	3 44	3 47	7 41	1128	1132	10 4	......	......	......
Bloomsbury to Barking	......	......	......	1 6	1 14	10 4	......	......	......
Barking to Bloomsbury........................	......	......	......	2 1	2 5	11 9	......	......	......
All-night service, Poplar—Bloomsbury.									

43. Car 1325 is about to reverse for its return trip to Smithfield on service 65. Note the handsome terrace of houses in the background. So much of this type of property disappeared in the Second World War, and many buildings which survived the Blitz failed to find a place in new post-war highway schemes and high rise housing estates. (W.A.Camwell)

44. We finish our ride eastwards at the change pit by Iron Bridge on the county boundary between London and Essex. Car 843 already has its pole up as it inches forward in the direction of Canning Town and the former West Ham tracks. This scene is also pictured in the *East Ham and West Ham Tramways* album. On the rocker panels of both trams is a notice explaining the curtailment of service 67 over the Easter period of 1940. (D.W.K.Jones)

December 1935.

67 BARKING — POPLAR — ALDGATE
Via East Ham, Upton Park, Canning Town, Poplar Stepney. Service interval, 2-4 minutes.
Journey time, 45 minutes. Through fare 5½d.
SPECIAL EARLY JOURNEYS ON SUNDAYS:
Blackwall Tunnel to Bloomsbury 4.51, 5.4, 6.2.
Bloomsbury to Blackwall Tunnel 5.27, 5.40, 6.32.
Bloomsbury to Barking 5.40.

Barking Bdy. to Aldgate	4 16	4 59	11 36	4 16	4 58	1 34	6 35	11 50	......
Barking Bdy. to Poplar (Blackwall Tunnel)	4 16	4 59	12 16	4 16	4 58	1 34	6 35	12 5	......
Aldgate to Barking Broadway	5 1	5 7	11 35	5 1	5 7	12 56	7 14	11 29	......
Aldgate to East Ham (Town Hall)	5 1	5 7	12 9	5 1	5 7	12 56	7 14	11 29	......
Aldgate to Poplar (Blackwall Tunnel)	5 1	5 7	12 18	5 1	5 7	2 12	7 14	12 32	......
Poplar (Aberfeldy St.) to Barking Broadway	3 50	4 45	11 52	3 50	4 45	1 12	6 12	11 45	......
Blackwall Tunnel to East Ham (Green Street)	5 19	5 25	12 31	5 19	5 25	1 11	6 11	12 29	......
All-night service, Poplar-Aldgate									

71 ALDERSGATE — WOOD GREEN — ALDGATE
Via Goswell Rd., Angel, Upper St., Highbury, Holloway, Finsbury Pk. Manor House, Wood Green, Lordship Lane Bruce Grove, Stamford Hill, Clapton, Hackney, Cambridge Heath, Whitechapel.
Service interval, 6 mins. Journey time, Aldgate—Wood Green 62 mins, Bruce Grove—Aldersgate 50 mins Aldgate — Aldersgate 95 mins.
Sundays, Aldgate—Wood Green only.
Service interval, 6 minutes.

Principal fares, Aldgate—Wood Green 7d.
Wood Green—Aldersgate 6d.

Aldersgate to Aldgate	7 3	7 9	1031	7 3	7 9	11 12	......	......	......
Aldersgate to Wood Green	7 3	7 9	1031	7 3	7 9	11 30	......	......	......
Aldgate to Aldersgate	5 31	5 54	9 12	5 31	5 54	9 57	......	......	......
Aldgate to Wood Green	4 43	5 31	1154	4 43	5 31	12 9	8 42	1132	......
Wood Green to Aldersgate	6 23	6 29	10 6	6 23	6 29	10 50	......	......	......
Wood Green to Aldgate	5 15	5 26	1155	5 15	5 26	12 0	8 53	1145	......
Wood Green to Hackney	5 15	5 26	1155	5 15	5 26	12 9	8 53	1226	......
Wood Green to Bruce Grove	4 50	5 15	1155	4 50	5 15	12 9	8 53	1226	......
Hackney to Wood Green	4 14	4 53	1213	4 14	4 53	12 45	8 21	1149	......
Hackney to Aldgate	4 24	5 13	1229	4 24	5 13	12 35	8 24	1217	......
Hackney to Stamford Hill	4 14	4 53	1257	4 14	4 53	1 13	8 21	1251	......
Stamford Hill to Hackney	5 35	5 46	1 19	5 35	5 46	1 29	8 37	1 9	......
Stamford Hill to Wood Green	4 28	5 7	1228	4 28	5 7	1 0	8 33	12 2	......
Bruce Grove to Wood Green	4 37	5 4	1237	4 37	5 4	1 9	8 42	1211	......
Bruce Grove to Hackney	5 26	5 37	1228	5 26	5 37	12 20	9 3	1237	......

BURDETT ROAD

45. Burdett Road was constructed in 1862 as a broad thoroughfare joining the East India and West India docks to Mile End Road. This postcard of a horse tram and early motor bus by Burdett Road Station is postmarked December 1906. The station was opened by the London and Blackwall Railway in September 1871 and it was closed by the LNER in April 1941. (J.H.Price Coll.)

46. Car 1260 was reconditioned by London Transport in June 1935 and it lasted until September 1950. Note the sandbags on the pavement and the headlamp mask on the tram. Trolleybus wires await the introduction of route 677 which will take place on 10th September 1939. The trams being railbound, have no trouble passing under the railway bridge, however, guide lights are necessary for trolleybus drivers. (C.G.Stevens)

ROUTE No. 12.
Cassland Road to West India Docks (Horse Traction).

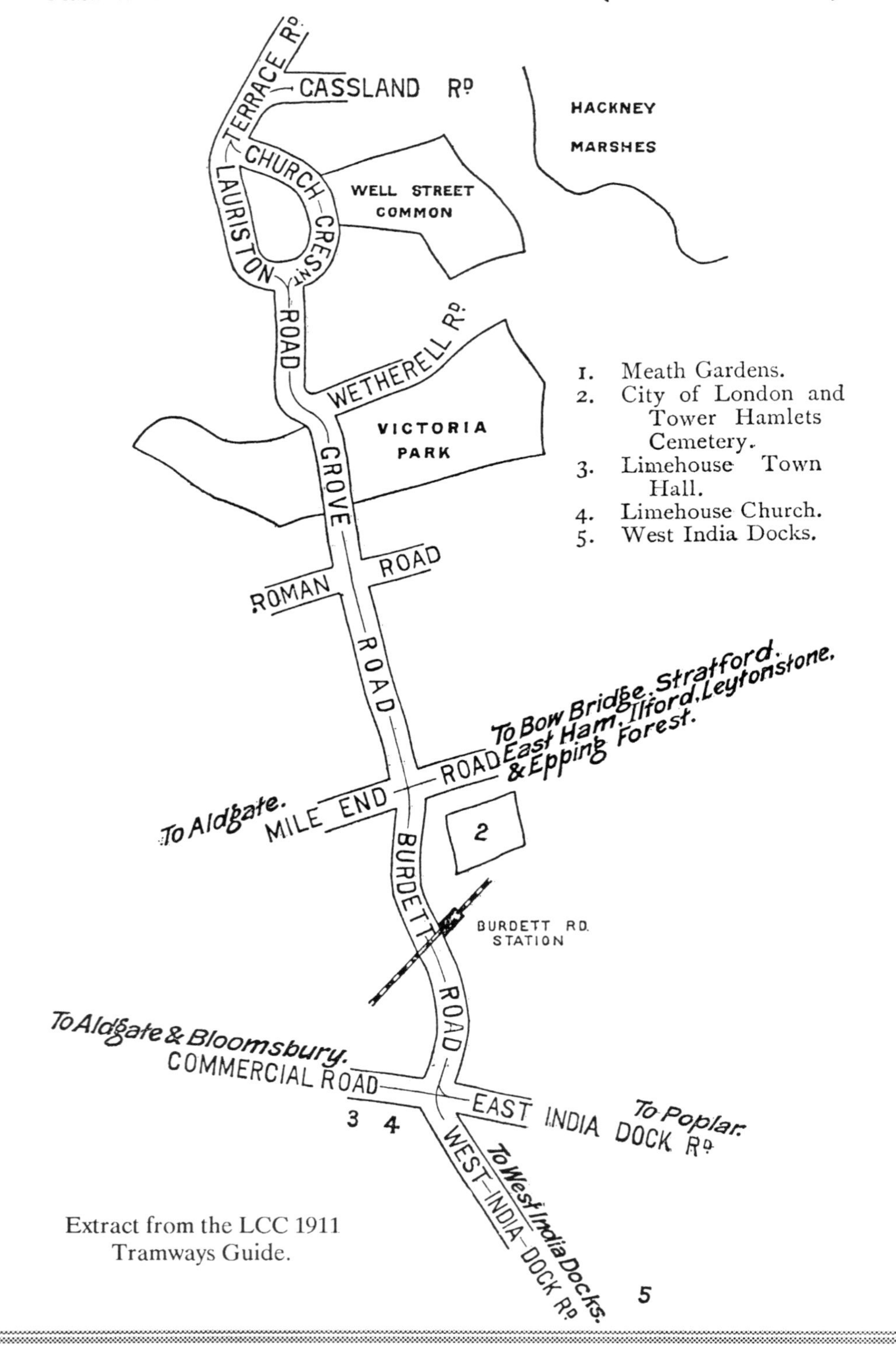

Extract from the LCC 1911 Tramways Guide.

47. A North Met. horse car passes the entrance to St.Dunstan's Road. This line was first opened on 1872/3 and it was worked by yellow painted cars. The service was short lived and it closed in June 1873. It was restored in 1879 as part of a through route to South Hackney. (B.J.Cross Coll.)

48. Burdett Road was named in honour of the famous victorian philanthropist, Baroness Angela Burdett Coutts. Here car 761 heads towards Mile End. (D.Jones Coll.)

49. Dazzling winter sunshine pierces the haze and seems about to consume this LCC tram on service 77 as it passes over splayed tracks at the northern end of Burdett Road. This form of layout with a public convenience situated between the "up" and "down" lines could also be found at several other locations in London. (H.Wightman)

December 1935.

Route	Description	Journey									
47	**STAMFORD HILL — LONDON DOCKS** Via Stoke Newington, Kingsland Rd., Shoreditch, Leman Street. Through fare 4d. Service interval 2-4 mins. Journey time, 30 mins.	**Stamford Hill** to London Docks	4 50	5 12	11 **44**	4 50	5 12	11 50	6 10	12 6	......
		London Docks to Stamford Hill	5 21	5 44	12 16	5 21	5 44	12 21	6 37	1235	......
49	**EDMONTON — DALSTON — LIVERPOOL ST.** Via Stamford Hill, Kingsland Rd., Shoreditch. Extended weekday rush hours & Sat. p.m. to Enfield. Service interval, Weekdays only, Liverpool St.—Edmonton 3-6 mins,. Edmonton—Enfield 6 mins. Journey time Liverpool St.—Edmonton 44 mins.,—Enfield 61 mins. Through fare 6d. * to Tramway Ave. † Later cars until 1133 to Stamford Hill. ‡ Earlier car, 5.38 from Stamford Hill.	**Edmonton** to Liverpool St. Stn	5 3	5 17	11 **23**	5 3	5 15	11 **26**	......	......	......
		Edmonton to Stamford Hill	5 3	5 17	1 0	5 3	5 15	1 0	......	......	......
		Liverpool St. Stn. to Edmonton	5 35	5 47	12* 7	5 35	5 47	12* 5	......	......	......
		Stamford Hill to Liverpool St. Stn	5 11	5 23	11 **42**	5 11	5 23	11 **47**	......	......	......
		Stamford Hill to Edmonton	4 41	4 53	12*29	4 41	4 53	12*28	......	......	......
		Liverpool St. Stn. to Enfield ......morning	5‡35	5 47	7 54	5‡35	5 47	7 42	......	......	......
		Liverpool St. Stn. to Enfield......afternoon	**4 24**	**4 30**	**6 30**	12 0	**12 6**	**10 30**	......	......	......
		Enfield to Liverpool St. Stn......morning	6 16	6 22	8 46	6 16	6 22	8 46	......	......	......
		Enfield to Liverpool St. Stn......afternoon	**4 47**	**4 53**	**7 35**	1147	1153	11† 9	......	......	......

MILE END TO STRATFORD

50. The horse tram emerging from Grove Road looks distinctly dated compared with its internal combustion engine and electric rivals. A West Ham car on a joint service works along Mile End Road in this 1913 view. (A.W.Ellis)

December 1935.

61 **LEYTON — STRATFORD — ALDGATE**
Via Whipps Cross, Leytonstone, Stratford, Bow, Mile End, Whitechapel.
Service interval 3-4 mins. Journey time, 47 mins.
Through fare 6d. * to Stratford.
SPECIAL LATE JOURNEYS :
Bow Bridge to Manor Park Broadway, 1.24 Mon.-Fri., 1.17 Sat., 1.18 Sun. Manor Park Broadway to Bow, 1.40 Mon.-Fri., 1.33 Sat., 1.34 Sun.

Leyton (Baker Arms) to Aldgate	4 36	4 52	**1145**	4 36	4 52	**1142**	8 17	11 47	......
Leyton (Bakers Arms) to Bow	4 36	4 52	1245	4 36	4 52	1236	8 17	12 36	......
Aldgate to Leyton (Bakers Arms)	5 10	5 26	**12 0**	5 10	5 26	1215	7 59	**12** 0	......
Aldgate to Bow	3 55	4 35	1230	3 55	4 35	1231	7* 7	12 30	......
Bow to Aldgate	3 36	4 15	1212	3 36	4 15	1210	6 50	12 15	......
Bow to Leyton (Bakers Arms)	5 14	5 26	1217	5 14	5 26	1232	8 14	12 15	......
Stratford to Aldgate	5 1	5 15	12 6	5 1	5 15	12 4	7 30	12 9	......
Stratford to Bow	5 1	5 15	1 49	5 1	5 15	1 42	7 30	1 42	......
Stratford to Leyton (Bakers Arms)	5 19	5 31	1223	5 19	5 31	1238	8 20	12 21	......

51. We take a front seat on the top deck of a car slowing for the crossing of lines from Burdett Road into Grove Road. Ahead is the change pit in Mile End Road where our tram will "shoot" its plough and then alter current collection to the trolley pole.
(G.N.Southerden)

52. The chemist on the corner offers the services of a surgeon dentist, whilst outside in the street, car 1188 brakes on the curve leading into Grove Road. (D.Jones Coll.)

53. As this view indicates, kerbside loading was possible outside the Prince of Wales, which meant that late night revellers did not have far to stagger to catch the tram. But times are changing, and trolleybus traction standards presage the arrival of a new era. (H.B.Priestley)

54. The West Ham car in the centre of this picture looks somewhat old fashioned when seen alongside its LCC fellow. In the background is Mile End Station, first served in 1905 by electric trains of the District Railway. (C.F.Klapper)

55. In the late 1930s work started on the Central Line extension from Liverpool Street to Stratford and Leytonstone. Here at Mile End the boring of new tube tunnels hit snags because of the porous nature of the soil. On the surface life goes on as normal inspite of the construction site spilling out from the station. A crew member approaches a former West Ham car now in LT red and cream livery. The bus department has obviously chosen this moment to get ahead in the race towards the City! (H.B.Priestley)

56. Running the change pit at Mile End was obviously a family affair as we can tell from the two attendants on the left. An ex-Leyton E3 class car rolls majestically towards the camera. Note the exposed track and the tie bars which kept the rails to gauge...a precise 1435mm, or as it was in those days, four feet eight and a half inches. (H.B.Priestley)

63
ALDGATE
BUCHANAN'S
"BLACK & WHITE"
SCOTCH WHISKY
TAYLOR, WALKER
CENTRAL LINE EXTENSION
MILE END STATION

61
ALDGATE
STATION

57. Much interest attends car 910 - a seemingly reluctant pioneer of the GB surface contact system employed by the LCC in 1908. In a moment a few more volunteers will be needed to get the tram moving again. (B.J.Cross Coll.)

G.B. Surface-Contact System.—One of the cheapest surface-contact systems to install is that known as the **G.B. surface-contact system,** so called from the initials of its inventors. It is in use in Lincoln. The conductor is a $1\frac{3}{16}$-inch steel cable placed in a glazed earthenware pipe, about 5 inches in diameter, which is laid underneath the track. This conductor practically takes the place of the trolley wire in the overhead system, and is supplied with current from the generating station in a similar manner. Immediately over the conductor, and at intervals of from 6 to 9 feet, are placed the studs, which are constructed so that, when a magnet carried on the car passes over them, a small floating armature is forced against the conductor and by making circuit with the cable the stud is energized.

Stud of the G.B. System. — Transverse and longitudinal sections through the stud of the G.B. system are shown in

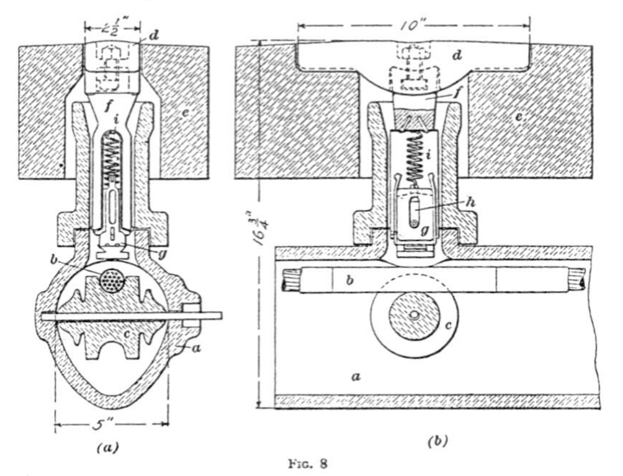

Fig. 8

Fig. 8 (*a*) and (*b*). The earthenware pipe *a* protects the conductor *b*, which is supported on the earthenware insulator *c*. Projecting downwards from a cast-iron stud head *d* set in a granite block *e* is a brass-lined cast-iron fork *f*. A galvanized-iron floating armature *g* works within this fork; its movement is limited by small pins that work in the slot *h*. The armature *g* carries a carbon contact-block held in a copper clip, and is normally kept from making contact with the conductor by a light spiral spring *i*. Flexible copper leads connect the copper clip with the main portion of the stud. When the car magnet passes over the stud, the lines of force pass through the stud and the forked projection to the steel conductor. The small floating armature sets itself against the pull of the spring *i*, so as to bridge the gap between the fork and the steel cable, and energizes the stud through the flexible copper connections. In order to prevent any injury to the strands of the working conductor through arcing at the switches, short sleeves of galvanized steel are slipped over the conductor throughout its whole length.

Working of the G.B. System. — The car equipment of the G.B. system consists, as usual, of a means of collecting the current and a magnet for operating the studs. The magnet is fixed rigidly to the car body and is connected to a storage battery carried on the car. The collector consists of a number of iron links suspended from a wire rope which takes the place of the usual rigid skate; when a stud is magnetized, these links are attracted and bear on the stud, thus conveying the current

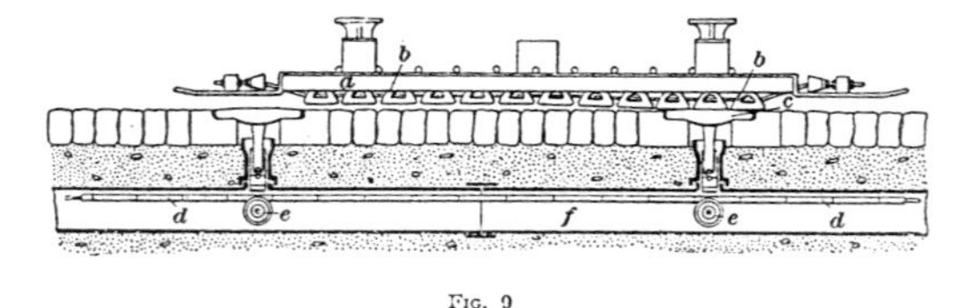

Fig. 9

to the car. When clear of the stud the links are drawn up out of the way of the paving. This arrangement allows the studs to be placed nearly flush with the roadway. In Fig. 9 is shown a longitudinal section of the collector. A rigid bar *a* running the whole length of the collector forms the magnet poles. It also supports the iron links *b*, which are attracted toward the stud *c*; *d* is the working conductor, *e* the supporting insulator, and *f* the earthenware pipe enclosing the conductor.

58. The line from Whitechapel Church to Bow was equipped with the GB set-up, which is explained in the accompanying technical article. Three trams had skates fixed underneath so that they could collect power. Unfortunately, in this case, necessity was the mother of a very poor invention and the whole operation which lasted from 25th June to 31st July 1908, descended into farce. In this rare view we look east along Bow Road to witness one of the ill fated "stud" cars about to make it past the Plough public house. (B.J.Cross Coll.)

59. Horse trams returned to Bow Road after the GB debacle and the line was eventually rebuilt with conduit to Mile End and trolley the rest of the way to Bow Bridge. (B.J.Cross Coll.)

60. On 31st July 1909 electric trams using overhead wires finally appeared in public service on Bow Road. Here E1 class car 1161 passes Coborn School. (B.J.Cross Coll.)

61. The parish church of St.Mary, Stratford-le-Bow, dates from 1311 and it has been added to and restored several times over the centuries. It stands by itself in this picture with the main highway and tramlines on either side. (B.J.Cross Coll.)

62. The connecting track to Bow Depot used to run along Fairfield Road. This July 1938 photo shows car 934 with the conductor on the rear platform. One of his jobs was to supervise the opening of the top deck windows so that passengers could feel more comfortable on this fine summer's day. (H.B.Priestley)

61
61
BARKING
65
ILFORD BDWY
14
15
16

QUEEN MARY'S HOSPITAL
63
ILFORD BDWY
63
94
5675
LOANS
DRESSING
PURDYS

63. Inside Bow Depot a couple of tramway enthusiasts pretend to be motormen as the photographer looks across the traverser pit. The traverser was a platform which moved sideways; it was a remarkably simple and efficient way of shunting trams about in LCC car sheds. The building seen here dates from 1908/10 and it was converted for trolleybuses in November 1939. Twenty years later motor buses took over and the depot still survives, albeit filled with diesel fumes! (W.A.Camwell)

65. St.John's Church, Stratford also occupies a central position between two highways. Here it looks down on car 191 which is loading passengers for the run to Leyton, Bakers Arms. It is hard to imagine such traffic free scenes nowadays. (H.B.Priestley)

64. Service 63 joined Bow to Stratford and these tracks are also described in companion album *East Ham and West Ham Tramways*. Car 94 later migrated south of the Thames to Abbey Wood Depot and here it stayed until the end of London's first generation tramway system in July 1952. (H.B.Priestley)

66. Above horse car 309 is the Great Eastern mainline to Liverpool Street Station. Below on Grove Road the passengers in this 1913 photo must have been wondering whether they would ever get a chance to ride an electric tram on this route. Overhead wires did go up in 1921, only after the tracks had been practically abandoned for seven years. (J.H.Price Coll.)

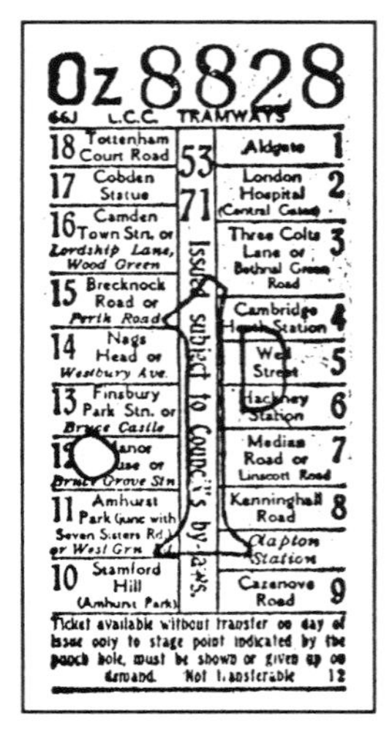

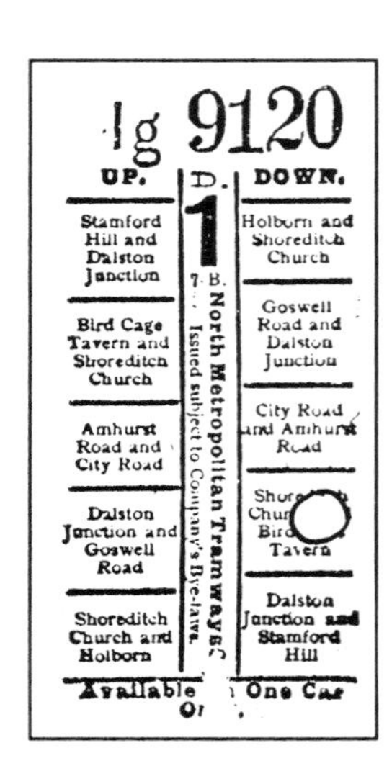

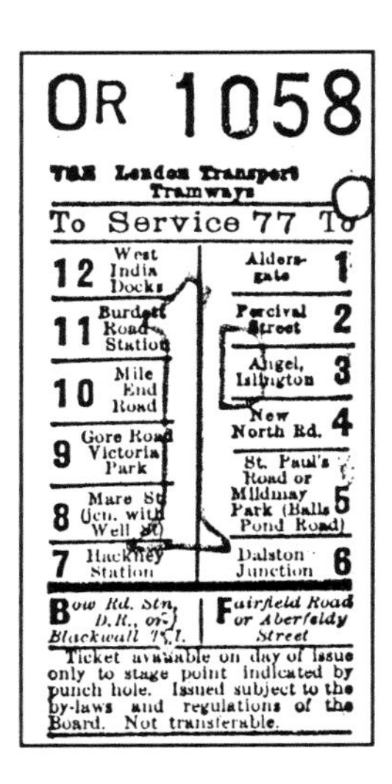

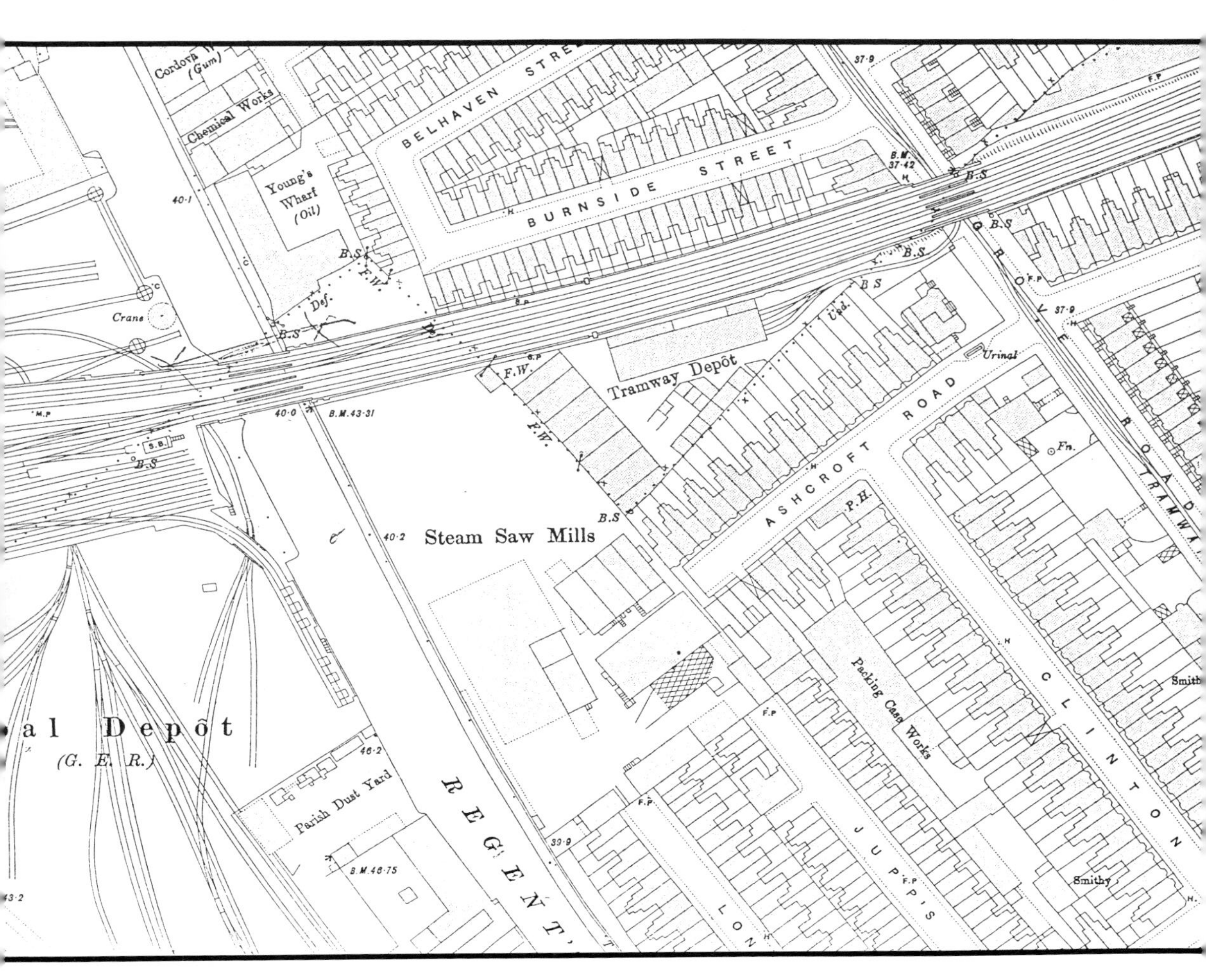

1898 edition

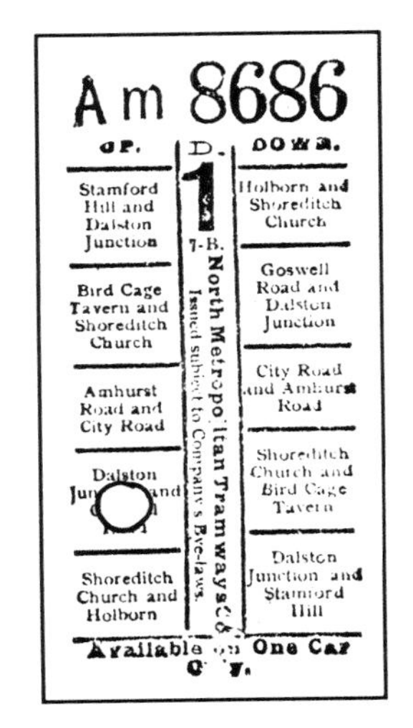

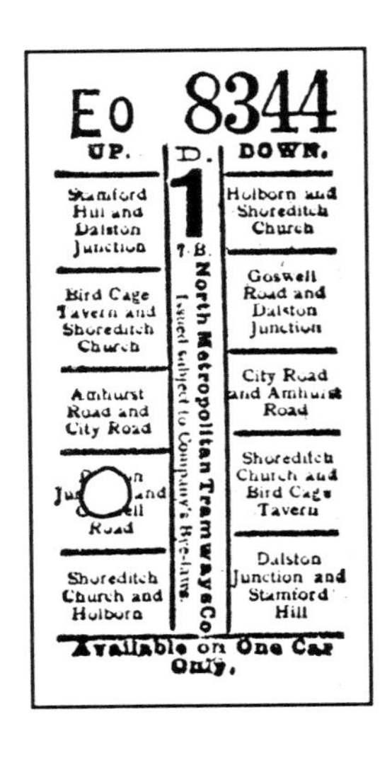

67. This part of Grove Road remained single track and loops after electrification. At the corner of Belhaven Street, car 1205 travels under the extra tram wires that have been added to the standard trolleybus array. (H.B.Priestley)

68. Outside the Baptist Church in Grove Road there was a skewed facing crossover in the horse tramway. In fact, the track to the left of the tram had fallen into disuse, and the hundred yards or so between Bunsen Street and St.Barnabas Church were designated single track to be used in both directions. (B.J.Cross Coll.)

69. Continuing the theme of permanent way oddities, we now observe a horse tram which has just negotiated a section of unusual double track in Lauriston Road. The two lines are laid very close together, hence it is impossible for two trams to pass. (B.J.Cross Coll.)

70. The conductor indicates with outstretched arm that his tram is about to veer to the left at the commencement of double track in Lauriston Road. The rails are now properly spaced in contrast with the previous eccentric horse car layout. In a couple of minutes this tram will reach Victoria Park, which was opened to the public by the LCC in 1895. (H.B.Priestley)

71. The replacing trolleybus standards are marked by two white bands. Car 1343 prepares to pull up by the post box in Church Crescent. This road was only used by northbound trams. (H.B.Priestley)

→ 72. This LCC tram has just crossed the southbound track and it now proceeds along Lauriston Road in the direction of Well Street. This arrangement of one way tram routes in adjacent streets is known to enthusiasts as "Cannon Hilling" after a particularly intricate example in Birmingham. (G.N.Southerden)

→ 73. Our round-the-houses tram tour of South Hackney ends with this view of car 1189 emerging from Terrace Road. The tram will shortly cross the northbound track in the foreground, and it will then run along Lauriston Road past the western end of St.John of Jerusalem's Church to rejoin the northbound track at the foot of Church Crescent. (H.B.Priestley)

77
ALDERSGATE

77
WEST INDIA DK
via DALSTON JUNC
REID'S SPECIAL STOUT

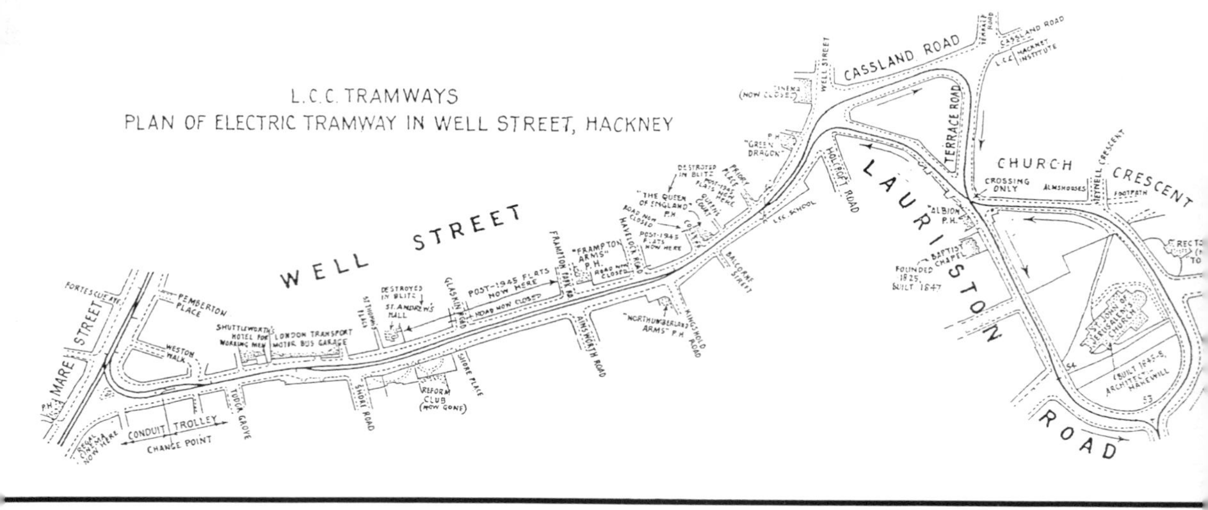

74. The old LCC tramway traction standards are now redundant and many await removal by the contractors who are installing the trolleybus wiring. Car 906 passes the entrance to Tudor Grove; in the background is the facade of Hackney Garage. This building was opened by the London General Omnibus Co. in June 1911 and it was closed by LT in April 1981. (H.B.Priestley)

75. The change pit from overhead trolley to conduit was situated at the end of Well Street. This is the first of three shots where we examine this interesting feature of London's tramways. (H.B.Priestley)

76. We move in closer to observe the attendant guiding the plough into the carrier under the tram. For this task he usually employed a fork shaped device whose tines fitted the channels of the plough carrier. Thus the plough was slid in place. The conduit system is fully described in *Embankment and Waterloo Tramways.* (H.B.Priestley)

77. The trolley pole has been lowered on the nearer tramcar and it is now ready to resume its journey using the conduit. A sister car has just "shot" its plough at the change pit and it continues along Well Street. (H.B.Priestley)

78. The electric tramway in Mare Street was opened in July 1909 and it replaced the horse car service which dated from 1873. A car on the circuitous service 53 heads towards Tottenham Court Road. On the right of the picture is the Lady Holle's School for Girls building which was constructed in 1877/78. (D.Jones Coll.)

79. Hackney Town Hall as it was at the turn of the century - this fine monument to municipal pride was started in 1864 and completed two years later. From the top deck of a well loaded horse tram, a number of local ratepayers can inspect their investment. (B.J.Cross Coll.)

80. There is a triangular junction where Graham Road meets Mare Street. These tracks were electrified in March 1913 and the west to south connecting curves were opened in December 1921. The car in the middle distance is working Service 81 to Bloomsbury via Essex Road. (D.Jones Coll.)

WEST INDIA DK.

Matthew Rose
DENTIST
BUNCH
&
DUKE
Auctioneers
358 LYONS

81. Car 881 slows to a halt at the eastern end of Graham Road. In this June 1939 view we catch a glimpse of the rear of a trolleybus in Mare Street; two motor buses and a taxi add to the variety of street transport. Note the facing crossover in the foreground. (H.B.Priestley)

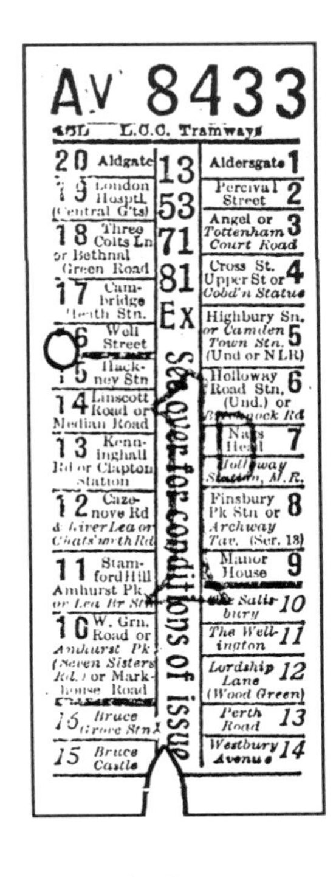

82. The trams worked a one way system in the centre of Hackney. Cars used Amhurst Road and Dalston Lane outbound; London bound trams were confined to the tracks seen here in Mare Street. A set of rails leads off to the right of the picture into Bohemia Place and Hackney Depot. (B.J.Cross Coll.)

83. This 1950s view of the depot approach shows the former car sheds which were converted in 1939 to house London Transport trolleybuses. The depot was renamed Clapton in 1950 to avoid confusion with Hackney bus garage in Well Street. Trolleybuses finished in April 1959 to be replaced by diesel powered vehicles which used the premises until closure in August 1987. (C.Carter)

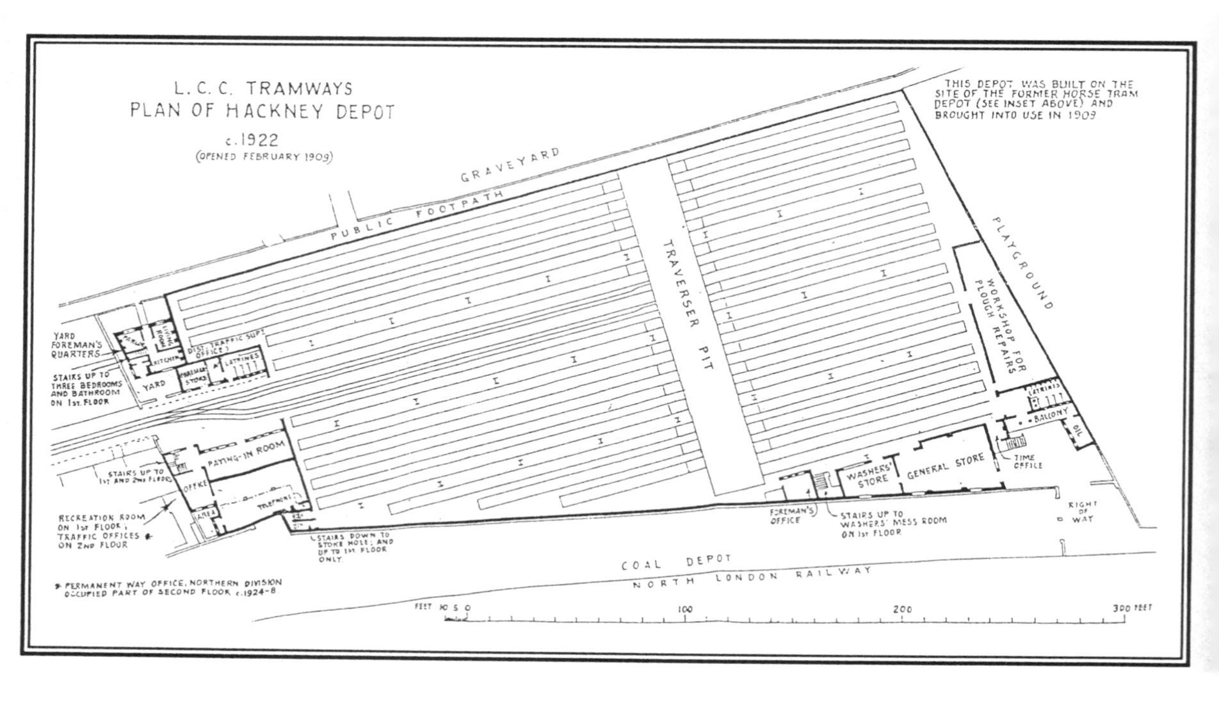

84. Residents of Hackney once had a direct tramway connection to South London via the Kingsway Subway. This facility lasted until 10th December 1939 when service 31 was cut back to terminate at Islington Green. Car 1959 is depicted here in Mare Street outside Marks and Spencer. (H.B.Priestley)

85. Mare Street was only just wide enough to accommodate this passing loop near the junction with Kenmure Road. It is probable that this horse tram is slowing gently to a halt in order to let a northbound car pass. (B.J.Cross)

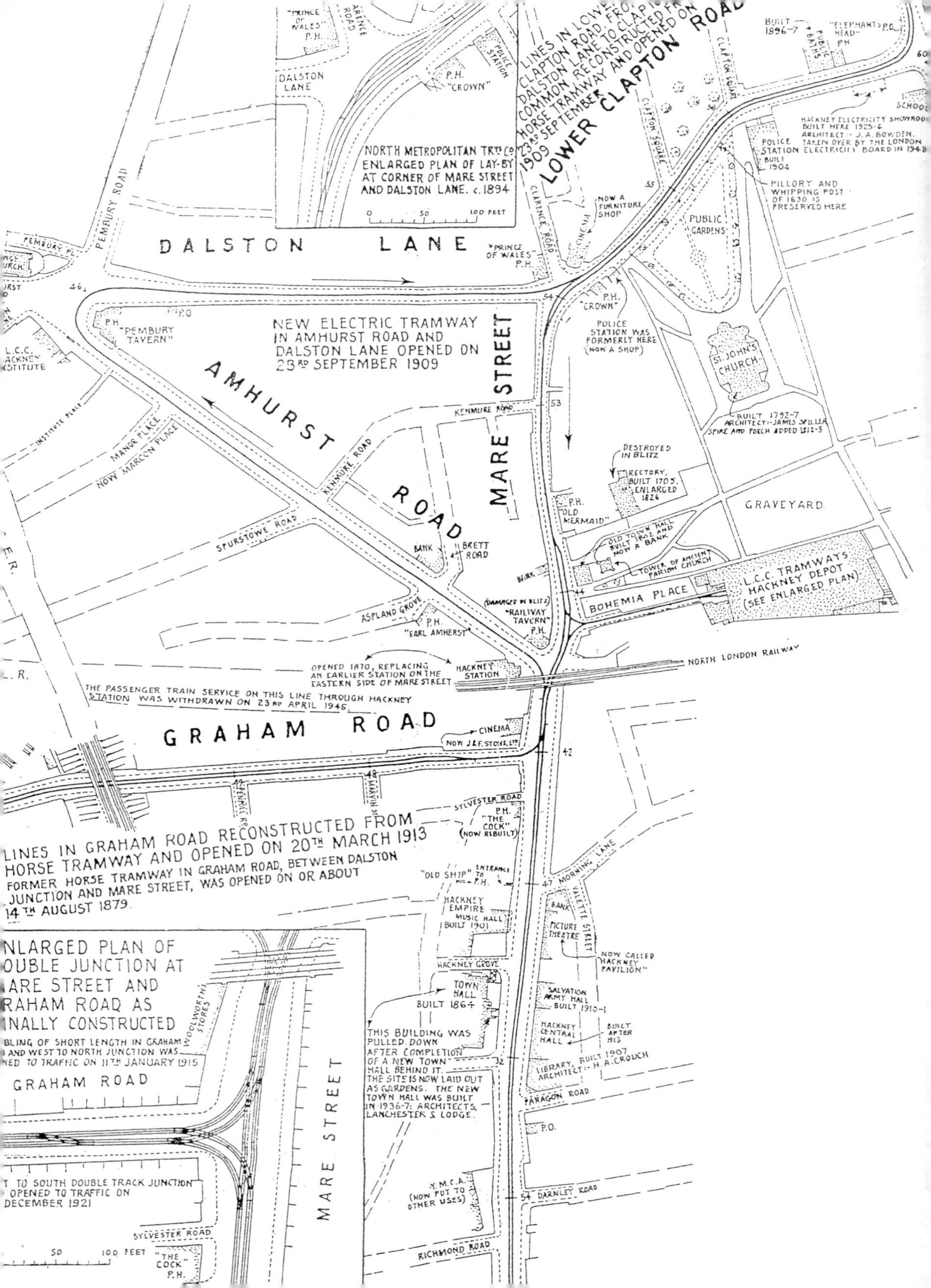
LINES IN LOWER CLAPTON ROAD, FROM DALSTON LANE TO CLAPTON COMMON RECONSTRUCTED FROM HORSE TRAMWAY AND OPENED ON 23RD SEPTEMBER 1909
LOWER CLAPTON ROAD
NORTH METROPOLITAN TRYS CO ENLARGED PLAN OF LAY-BY AT CORNER OF MARE STREET AND DALSTON LANE. c. 1894
0 50 100 FEET
"PRINCE OF WALES" P.H.
DALSTON LANE
P.H. "CROWN"
POLICE STATION
CLARENCE ROAD
CLAPTON SQUARE
BUILT 1896-7
PUBLIC BATHS
"ELEPHANTS HEAD" P.H.
P.O.
SCHOOL
HACKNEY ELECTRICITY SHOWROOM BUILT HERE 1925-6 ARCHITECT:- J. A. BOWDEN. TAKEN OVER BY THE LONDON ELECTRICITY BOARD IN 1948
POLICE STATION BUILT 1904
PILLORY AND WHIPPING POST OF 1630 IS PRESERVED HERE
NOW A FURNITURE SHOP
CINEMA
PUBLIC GARDENS
PEMBURY ROAD
PEMBURY PL.
DALSTON LANE
"PRINCE OF WALES" P.H.
P.H. "CROWN"
POLICE STATION WAS FORMERLY HERE (NOW A SHOP)
ST. JOHN'S CHURCH
BUILT 1792-7 ARCHITECT:- JAMES SPILLER SPIRE AND PORCH ADDED 1812-3
P.H. "PEMBURY TAVERN"
P.O.
L.C.C. HACKNEY INSTITUTE
NEW ELECTRIC TRAMWAY IN AMHURST ROAD AND DALSTON LANE OPENED ON 23RD SEPTEMBER 1909
AMHURST ROAD
MARE STREET
KENMURE ROAD
INSTITUTE PLACE
MANOR PLACE
NOW MARCON PLACE
DESTROYED IN BLITZ
RECTORY, BUILT 1705 ENLARGED 1826
P.H. "OLD MERMAID"
GRAVEYARD
OLD TOWN HALL BUILT 1802 AND NOW A BANK
TOWER OF ANCIENT PARISH CHURCH
L.C.C. TRAMWAYS HACKNEY DEPOT (SEE ENLARGED PLAN)
BOHEMIA PLACE
SPURSTOWE ROAD
BANK
BRETT ROAD
BANK
(DAMAGED IN BLITZ) "RAILWAY TAVERN" P.H.
ASPLAND GROVE
P.H. "EARL AMHERST"
OPENED 1870, REPLACING AN EARLIER STATION ON THE EASTERN SIDE OF MARE STREET
HACKNEY STATION
NORTH LONDON RAILWAY
THE PASSENGER TRAIN SERVICE ON THIS LINE THROUGH HACKNEY STATION WAS WITHDRAWN ON 23RD APRIL 1945
GRAHAM ROAD
CINEMA NOW J.&F. STONE, LTD.
SYLVESTER ROAD
P.H. "THE COCK" (NOW REBUILT)
MARVIN ST.
LINES IN GRAHAM ROAD RECONSTRUCTED FROM HORSE TRAMWAY AND OPENED ON 20TH MARCH 1913
FORMER HORSE TRAMWAY IN GRAHAM ROAD, BETWEEN DALSTON JUNCTION AND MARE STREET, WAS OPENED ON OR ABOUT 14TH AUGUST 1879.
"OLD SHIP" ENTRANCE TO P.H.
MORNING LANE
HACKNEY EMPIRE MUSIC HALL BUILT 1901
BANK
PICTURE THEATRE
VALETTE STREET
NOW CALLED HACKNEY PAVILION
HACKNEY GROVE
TOWN HALL BUILT 1864
THIS BUILDING WAS PULLED DOWN AFTER COMPLETION OF A NEW TOWN HALL BEHIND IT. THE SITE IS NOW LAID OUT AS GARDENS. THE NEW TOWN HALL WAS BUILT IN 1936-7: ARCHITECTS, LANCHESTER & LODGE.
SALVATION ARMY HALL BUILT 1910-1
HACKNEY CENTRAL HALL
BUILT AFTER 1913
LIBRARY, BUILT 1907 ARCHITECT:- H.A. CROUCH
PARAGON ROAD
P.O.
Y.M.C.A. (NOW PUT TO OTHER USES)
DARNLEY ROAD
RICHMOND ROAD
NLARGED PLAN OF OUBLE JUNCTION AT ARE STREET AND RAHAM ROAD AS INALLY CONSTRUCTED
BLING OF SHORT LENGTH IN GRAHAM AND WEST TO NORTH JUNCTION WAS NED TO TRAFFIC ON 11TH JANUARY 1915
WOOLWORTH STORES
GRAHAM ROAD
MARE STREET
T TO SOUTH DOUBLE TRACK JUNCTION OPENED TO TRAFFIC ON DECEMBER 1921
SYLVESTER ROAD
50 100 FEET
"THE COCK" P.H.

86. On 11th June 1939 most of Hackney's trams were replaced by trolleybuses, leaving only services 77 and 31 to eke out their remaining days. This 31 tram is seen terminating at the corner of Clarence Road and Dalston Lane. The Brooke and Sons furniture store behind the tram had once served as Hackney's very own Picture Palace. (H.B.Priestley)

87. The somewhat restricted dimensions of Mare Street encouraged the London County Council to lay this one way track in Dalston Lane, which was opened in September 1909. A good example of an LCC clover leaf stop sign stands on the pavement outside the Prince of Wales. A description of stop signs is included in *Victoria and Lambeth Tramways*. (J.H.Price Coll.)

88. We look from Urswick Road into Lower Clapton Road in time to witness car 1208 resplendent in its purple lake and primrose livery. The fleet number and the letters LCC on the side were painted in gold. (D.Jones Coll.)

89. LCC car 1190 pauses for the camera. On the other side of Lower Clapton Road the opposition poaches passengers who want to travel in the Leyton direction. However, when the heavens open, the electric trams have the advantage of a fully enclosed top deck, a facility this early motor bus could not match. (D.Jones Coll.)

LOWER CLAPTON

90. Our tramway exploration of the borough now leads us further along Lower Clapton Road. Here at the corner of Laura Place we stop awhile to view an approaching horse car on this sunny day long ago. This scene from times past evokes comparison with the staid, genteel world of Mr.Charles Pooter as immortalised by George and Weedon Grossmith in *The Diary of a Nobody,* published in 1894. (J.H.Price Coll.)

91. A North Metropolitan horse car halts by Clapton Pond. The date is the mid 1880s and this solid looking vehicle was delivered from John Stephenson and Co. of New York in 1871. Inside the lower saloon there were spaces for 22 people on two facing longitudinal benches; on the top deck a "knifeboard" back to back bench had room for another 22 passengers. (R.J.Harley Coll.)

Extract from the LCC 1911 Tramways Guide.

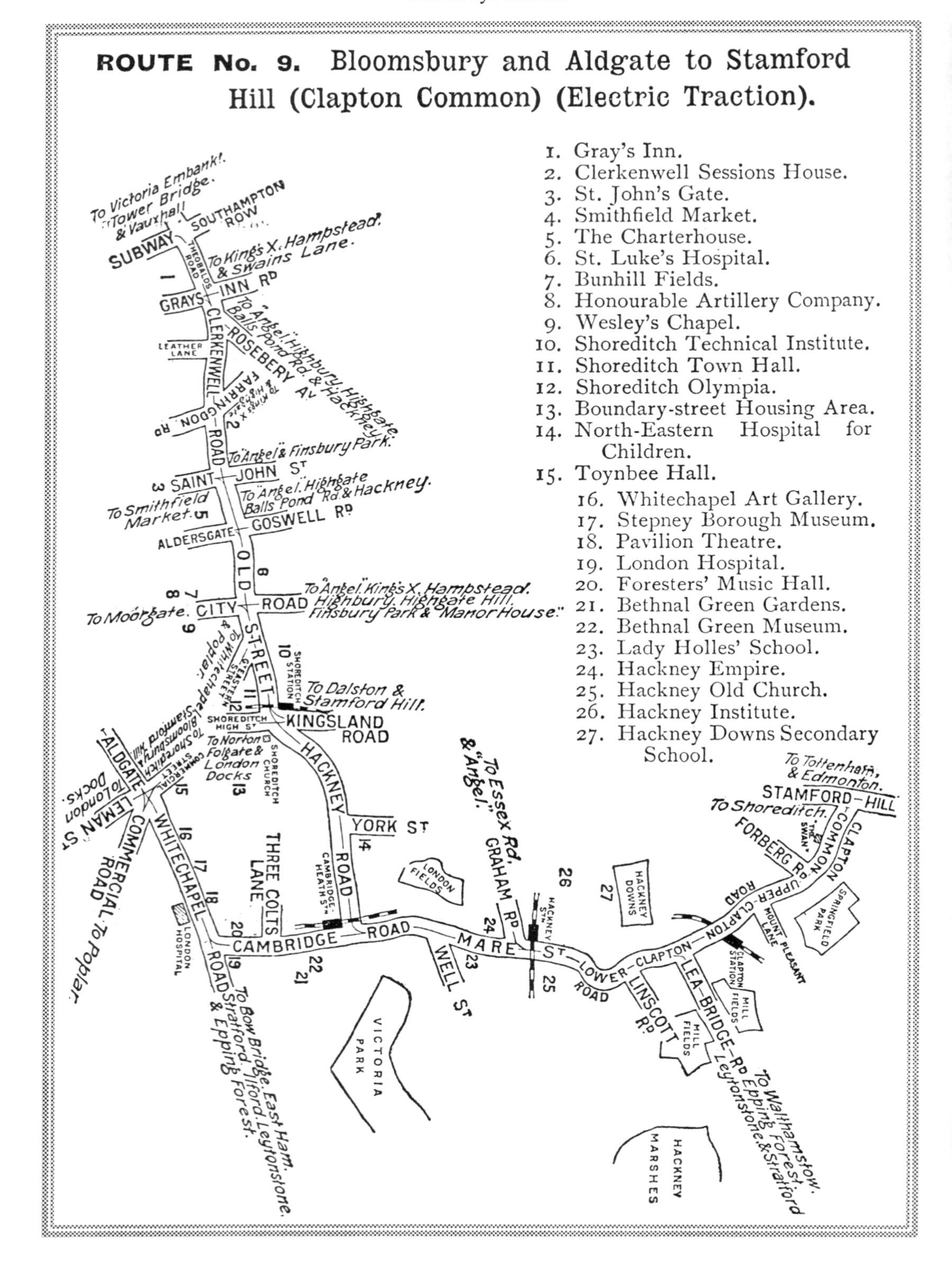

92. The negative of this photograph has been restored to reveal this classic scene from around 1906. In barely three years the clip-clop of horse cars will be but a memory on Lower Clapton Road. Note the children's clothes in an era when hats were deemed an essential fashion accessory. (B.J.Cross Coll.)

93. A Yates and Sons delivery tricycle crosses the tramlines in front of an immaculate, white painted LCC horse car. The photographer is standing with his back to Lea Bridge Road. Another view taken at this location is featured in companion album *Walthamstow and Leyton Tramways*. (J.H.Price Coll.)

HACKNEY TO SHOREDITCH

94. We leave the delights of Lower Clapton and we now head south towards Central London. This is the Triangle, Hackney as it appeared before the First World War. The site marks the location of several toll bars which collected their last dues on 30th June 1864. (D.Jones Coll.)

95. Cars 602 and 606 have been included by the postcard publisher in this view of Hackney Road, Cambridge Heath. The presence of these LCC electric trams was a source of pride for the locals and an enhancement to the modernity of the district. The railway bridge leading to Cambridge Heath Station on the Great Eastern is glimpsed in the background. Electrification of the tramways caused heavy losses of passenger traffic and revenue for the suburban railways. (B.J.Cross Coll.)

96. On the boundary between the two former Metropolitan Boroughs of Bethnal Green and Shoreditch, car 611 enters the single track by the Children's Hospital. The desperate living conditions in the surrounding area have been graphically described by the Poplar born novelist, Arthur Morrison (1863-1945), in *A Child of the Jago*, and *Tales of Mean Streets.* (B.J.Cross Coll.)

97. At the crossroads of Shoreditch High Street, Hackney Road, Kingsland Road and Old Street, a completely new track layout was installed in 1927/28. Here we see car 647 on the right of the picture, it is bound for Bloomsbury on service 55. Crossing its path is car 795 on service 49 to Liverpool Street. (G.N.Southerden)

98. The imposing Parish Church of St.Leonard, Shoreditch High Street, was erected in 1736-40. Below the 192 ft./58 metres tall steeple a horse tram on the Lea Bridge Road to Bloomsbury service, rattles over the crossing. (J.H.Price Coll.)

99. A grim day in January 1934 is enlivened by the antics of the tramways inspector. He has obviously devised his own programme of callisthenics to alleviate the boredom of supervising car movements at the southern end of Kingsland Road. A permanent way workman looks benignly into the camera, no doubt well aware of the foibles of his superiors! (H.Nicol)

100. Trams and street markets went together, and from Beresford Square to Whitechapel, the new electric cars brought business to the market traders. Here at Shoreditch browsers peruse the book bargains whilst the reliable 47 tramcars pass in the background.
(J.H.Price Coll.)

101. Car 1312 stops outside the Olympia Music Hall in Shoreditch High Street. Just past the tram on the right hand side is the start of Bethnal Green Road, one of the few local thoroughfares never to carry trams.
(D.Jones Coll.)

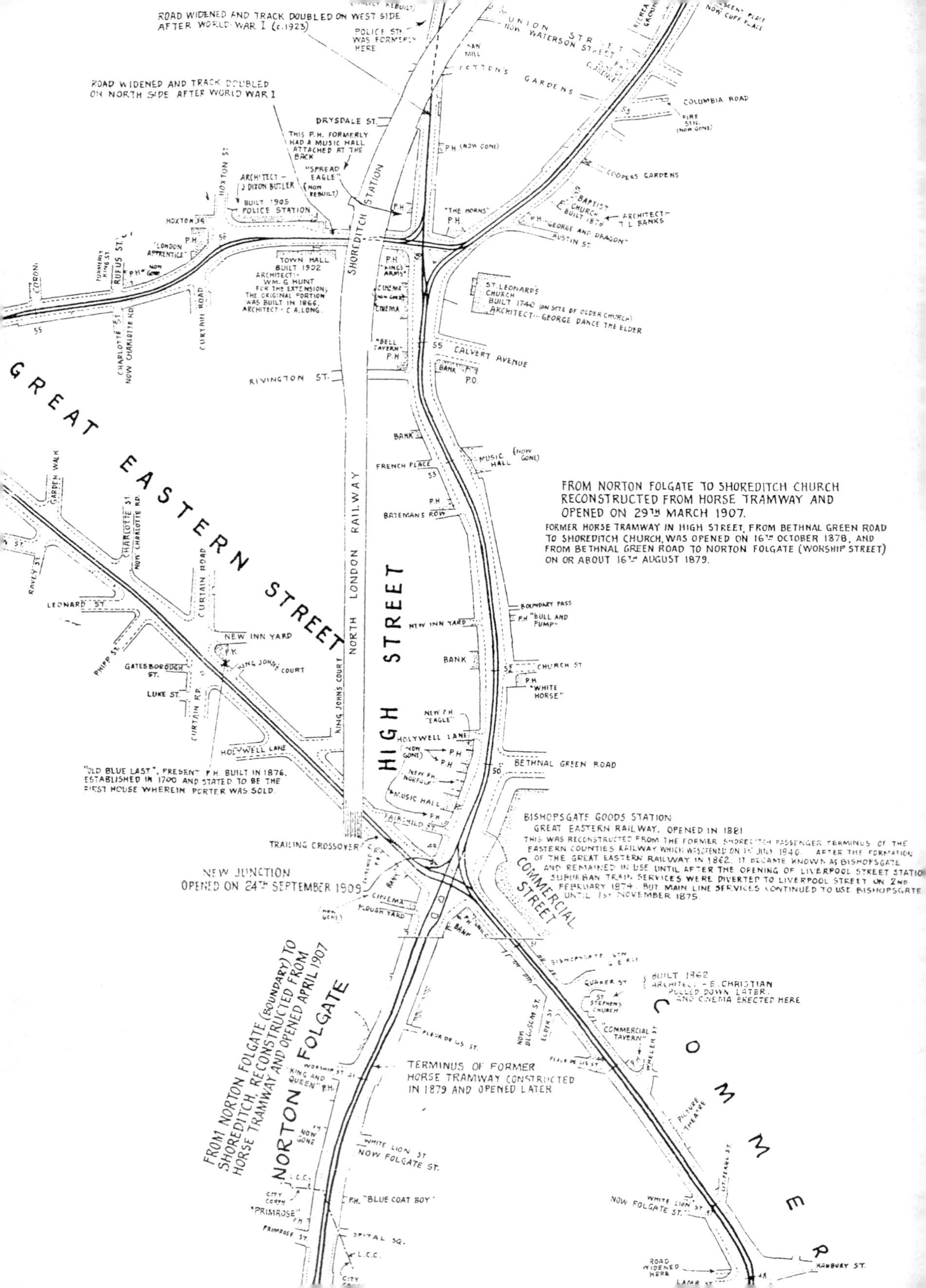

ROAD WIDENED AND TRACK DOUBLED ON WEST SIDE AFTER WORLD WAR I (c.1923)
POLICE STN WAS FORMERLY HERE
UNION STREET NOW WATERSON STREET
NOW CUFF PLACE
COTTON'S GARDENS
ROAD WIDENED AND TRACK DOUBLED ON NORTH SIDE AFTER WORLD WAR I
COLUMBIA ROAD
FIRE STN. (NOW GONE)
DRYSDALE ST.
THIS P.H. FORMERLY HAD A MUSIC HALL ATTACHED AT THE BACK
"SPREAD EAGLE" (NOW REBUILT)
P.H. (NOW GONE)
COOPERS GARDENS
HOXTON ST.
ARCHITECT - J. DIXON BUTLER
BUILT 1905 POLICE STATION
SHOREDITCH STATION
"THE HORNS" P.H.
BAPTIST CHURCH BUILT 1878
ARCHITECT - T. L. BANKS
P.H. "GEORGE AND DRAGON"
AUSTIN ST.
HOXTON
"LONDON APPRENTICE" P.H.
RUFUS ST.
FORMERLY KING ST.
CORONET
TOWN HALL BUILT 1902
ARCHITECT:- WM. G. HUNT FOR THE EXTENSION; THE ORIGINAL PORTION WAS BUILT IN 1866, ARCHITECT:- C. A. LONG.
P.H. "KINGS ARMS"
CINEMA
ST. LEONARD'S CHURCH BUILT 1740 (ON SITE OF OLDER CHURCH) ARCHITECT:- GEORGE DANCE THE ELDER
CHARLOTTE ST. NOW CHARLOTTE RD.
CURTAIN ROAD
"BELL TAVERN" P.H.
CALVERT AVENUE
BANK
P.O.
RIVINGTON ST.
GREAT EASTERN STREET
BANK
MUSIC HALL (NOW GONE)
FRENCH PLACE
GARDEN WALK
P.H.
BATEMANS ROW
NORTH LONDON RAILWAY
FROM NORTON FOLGATE TO SHOREDITCH CHURCH RECONSTRUCTED FROM HORSE TRAMWAY AND OPENED ON 29TH MARCH 1907.
FORMER HORSE TRAMWAY IN HIGH STREET, FROM BETHNAL GREEN ROAD TO SHOREDITCH CHURCH, WAS OPENED ON 16TH OCTOBER 1878, AND FROM BETHNAL GREEN ROAD TO NORTON FOLGATE (WORSHIP STREET) ON OR ABOUT 16TH AUGUST 1879.
CHARLOTTE ST. NOW CHARLOTTE RD.
CURTAIN ROAD
RAVEY ST.
LEONARD ST.
HIGH STREET
BOUNDARY PASS
P.H. "BULL AND PUMP"
NEW INN YARD
NEW INN YARD
PHIPP ST.
GATESBOROUGH ST.
KING JOHNS COURT
BANK
CHURCH ST.
P.H. "WHITE HORSE"
LUKE ST.
CURTAIN RD.
KING JOHNS COURT
NEW P.H. "EAGLE"
HOLYWELL LANE
HOLYWELL LANE
(NOW GONE) P.H.
BETHNAL GREEN ROAD
"OLD BLUE LAST", PRESENT P.H. BUILT IN 1876. ESTABLISHED IN 1700 AND STATED TO BE THE FIRST HOUSE WHEREIN PORTER WAS SOLD.
NEW P.H. NORFOLK
MUSIC HALL
P.H.
FAIRCHILD ST.
BISHOPSGATE GOODS STATION
GREAT EASTERN RAILWAY, OPENED IN 1881
THIS WAS RECONSTRUCTED FROM THE FORMER SHOREDITCH PASSENGER TERMINUS OF THE EASTERN COUNTIES RAILWAY WHICH WAS OPENED ON 1ST JULY 1840. AFTER THE FORMATION OF THE GREAT EASTERN RAILWAY IN 1862, IT BECAME KNOWN AS BISHOPSGATE AND REMAINED IN USE UNTIL AFTER THE OPENING OF LIVERPOOL STREET STATION. SUBURBAN TRAIN SERVICES WERE DIVERTED TO LIVERPOOL STREET ON 2ND FEBRUARY 1874, BUT MAIN LINE SERVICES CONTINUED TO USE BISHOPSGATE UNTIL 1ST NOVEMBER 1875.
TRAILING CROSSOVER
NEW JUNCTION OPENED ON 24TH SEPTEMBER 1909
BANK
CINEMA
PLOUGH YARD
COMMERCIAL STREET
BANK
BISHOPSGATE STN. G.E.RLY.
QUAKER ST.
BUILT 1862 ARCHITECT - E. CHRISTIAN PULLED DOWN LATER, AND CINEMA ERECTED HERE
ST. STEPHENS CHURCH
FROM NORTON FOLGATE (BOUNDARY) TO SHOREDITCH, RECONSTRUCTED FROM HORSE TRAMWAY AND OPENED APRIL 1907
NORTON FOLGATE
FLEUR DE LIS ST.
NOW BLOSSOM ST.
ELDER ST.
"COMMERCIAL TAVERN"
WHEELER ST.
FLEUR DE LIS ST.
WORSHIP ST.
"KING AND QUEEN" P.H.
TERMINUS OF FORMER HORSE TRAMWAY CONSTRUCTED IN 1879 AND OPENED LATER
COMMER
PICTURE THEATRE
P.H. NOW GONE
WHITE LION ST NOW FOLGATE ST.
L.C.C.
CITY CORPN
P.H. "BLUE COAT BOY"
WHITE LION ST. NOW FOLGATE ST.
"PRIMROSE" P.H.
PRIMROSE ST.
SPITAL SQ.
L.C.C.
CITY
ROAD WIDENED HERE
HANBURY ST.
LAMB ST.

102. In Norton Folgate a fair queue builds up before it can cross into Great Eastern Street or Shoreditch High Street. Note the "cannon" type cast iron bollards on the traffic island. (H.B.Priestley)

103. Car 1339 is caught by the camera at the foot of Great Eastern Street, it is about to turn north into Shoreditch High Street to regain its normal route along Hackney Road. Service 55's usual approach to Shoreditch was via Old Street. (B.J.Cross Coll.)

104. On 8th June 1907 there is still an air of excitement surrounding the latest electric trams. Cars 719 and 622, are depicted in sparkling condition, and they represent "the state of the art" as regards contemporary tramcar construction.
(National Tramway Museum)

BISHOPSGATE, LIVERPOOL STREET STATION

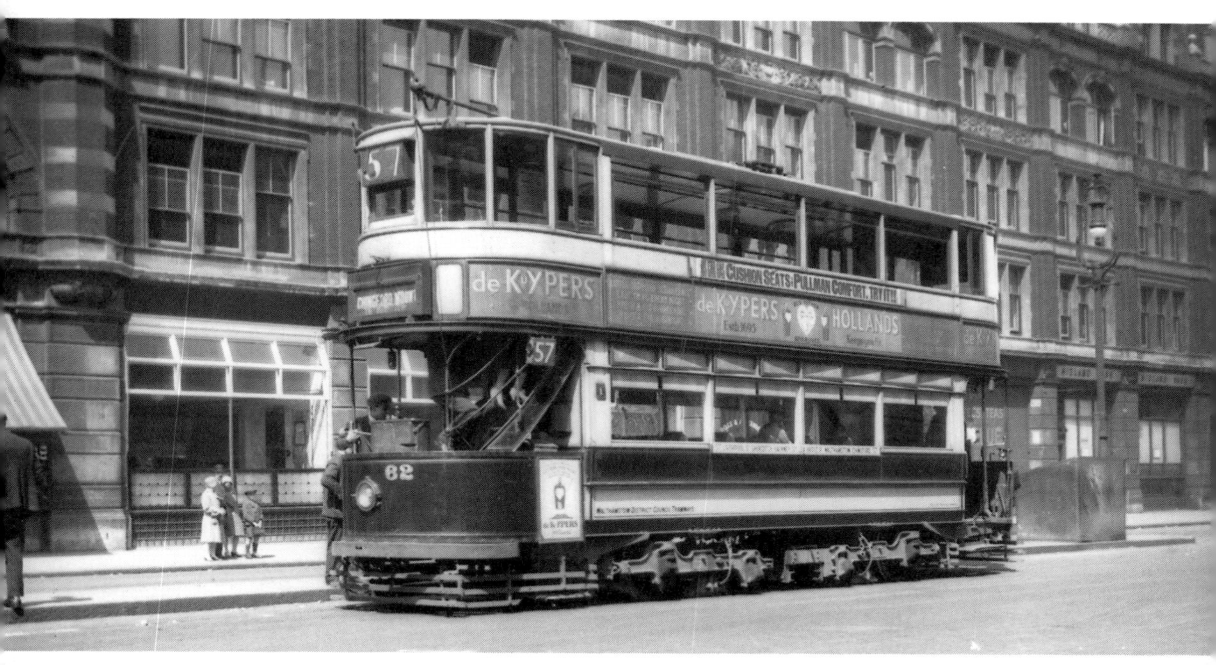

105. Walthamstow car 62 waits at the terminus on 5th August 1929 before the journey to Chingford Mount on joint service 57. The section of track from the LCC boundary in Norton Folgate to the corner of Bishopsgate and Middlesex Street in the City, opened on Good Friday 1913. (G.N.Southerden)

106. We end our tramway trip round East London with this view of lone car 571 at the end of the line by Liverpool Street Station. Very soon the construction crews will arrive with all the trolleybus paraphernalia, and the tramcar will pass into history. (W.A.Camwell)

ROLLING STOCK
Horse Cars

107. This close up of a Stephenson seven window car, part of a batch ordered by the North Metropolitan Company in 1871, shows clearly how well maintained these vehicles were. Later on, some trams had their upper deck knifeboard benches replaced by transverse "garden" type seats. (J.H.Price Coll.)

108. The LCC retained this horse car as part of the fleet needed for the West India Docks to South Hackney service. It is of lighter construction than the tramcar featured in the previous view. Although externally it looks in good condition, at the time of this photo, it could truly be said to be well past its "sell by date"! (LCC official photo)

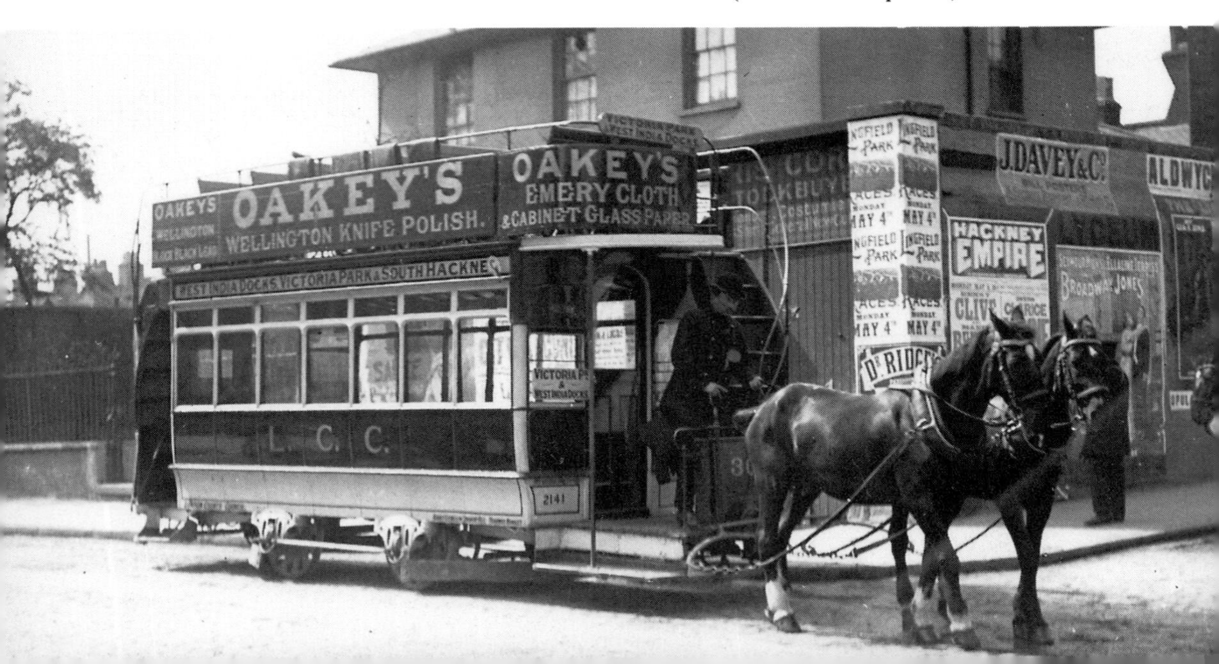

LCC class E

Cars 402-551, 602-751. These vehicles were the first to embody what became the "traditional" shape of the LCC tramcar. They were built in 1905/6 by Hurst, Nelson and they rode on Mountain and Gibson maximum traction trucks. One of these trucks is described in detail in the accompanying article from a 1908 tramways reference book. Each tram had seats for 76 passengers and the cars were delivered in the standard LCC purple lake and primrose livery. In 1927-30 vehicles of the E class were upgraded in a "Pullmanisation" programme which entailed the fitting of more comfortable seats and improvements to the interior decor. A new crimson red and cream livery was also applied to enhance the public perception of the vehicles. All cars passed to London Transport in July 1933 and they received the familiar LT red and cream livery. However, the future did not look bright and in March 1935 car 404 was scrapped by Cohens at Charlton Works. Mass scrapping of the class took place in the 1936-38 period as the trolleybus conversion gained momentum.

109. Car 712 is seen in pristine condition shortly after delivery. This car did not come equipped with trolley poles, thus confining it to conduit routes. Only cars 402-511 were fitted with trolleys. The original purple lake livery weathered over the years to a dull brown colour. (LCC official photo)

110. Car 531 is its final LT state before it is sent for scrapping in July 1938. Note the three line destination box so typical of cars working on the Hampstead services. (D.W.K.Jones)

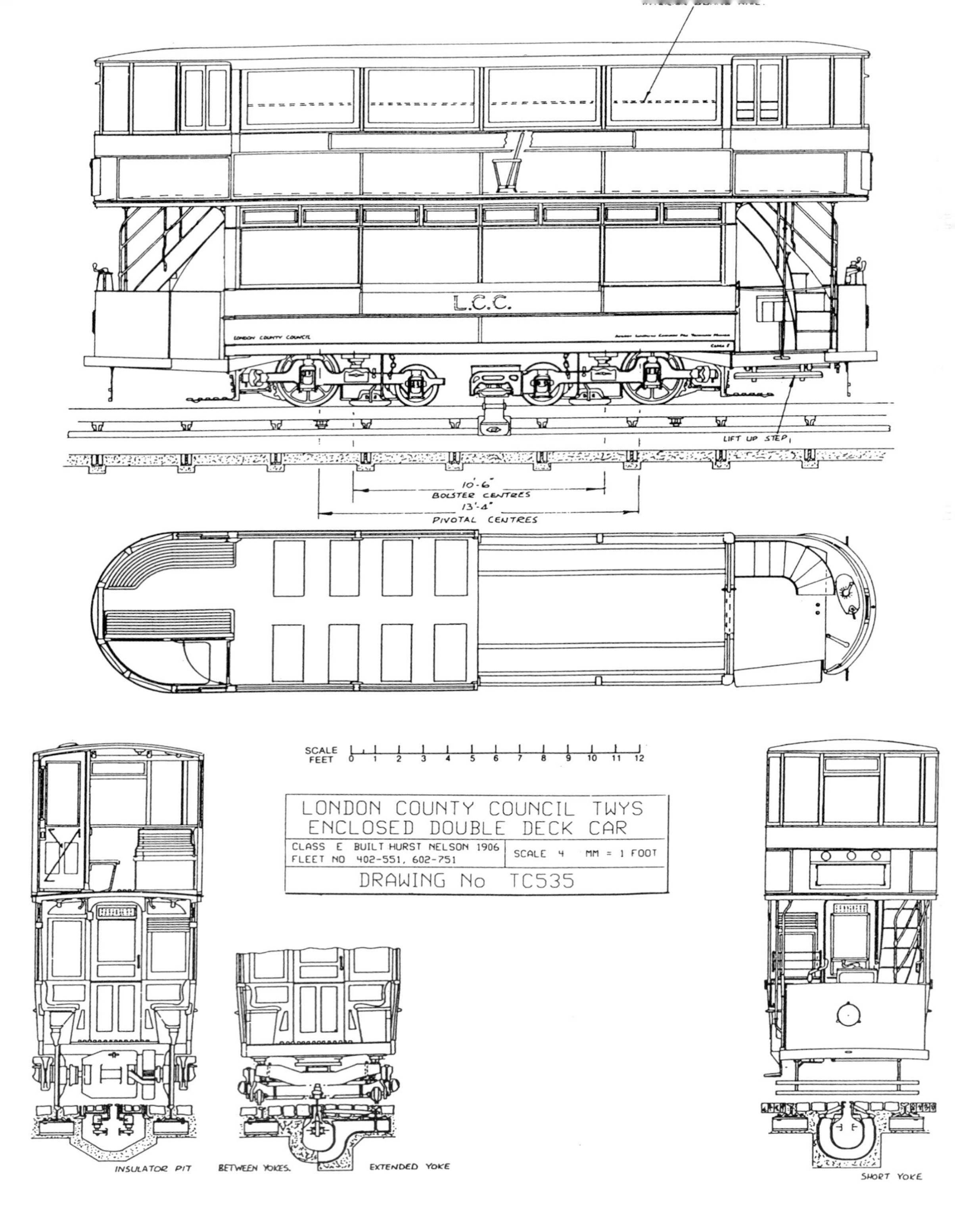

L.C.C.
LONDON COUNTY COUNCIL
LIFT UP STEP
10'-6"
BOLSTER CENTRES
13'-4"
PIVOTAL CENTRES
SCALE
FEET 0 1 2 3 4 5 6 7 8 9 10 11 12
LONDON COUNTY COUNCIL TWYS
ENCLOSED DOUBLE DECK CAR
CLASS E BUILT HURST NELSON 1906
FLEET NO 402-551, 602-751
SCALE 4 MM = 1 FOOT
DRAWING No TC535
INSULATOR PIT
BETWEEN YOKES.
EXTENDED YOKE
SHORT YOKE
DRAWN BY:-TERRY RUSSELL, "CHACESIDE", ST.LEONARDS PARK, HORSHAM, W.SUSSEX. RH13 6EG.
SEND 3 FIRST CLASS STAMPS FOR COMPLETE LIST OF PUBLIC TRANSPORT DRAWINGS.

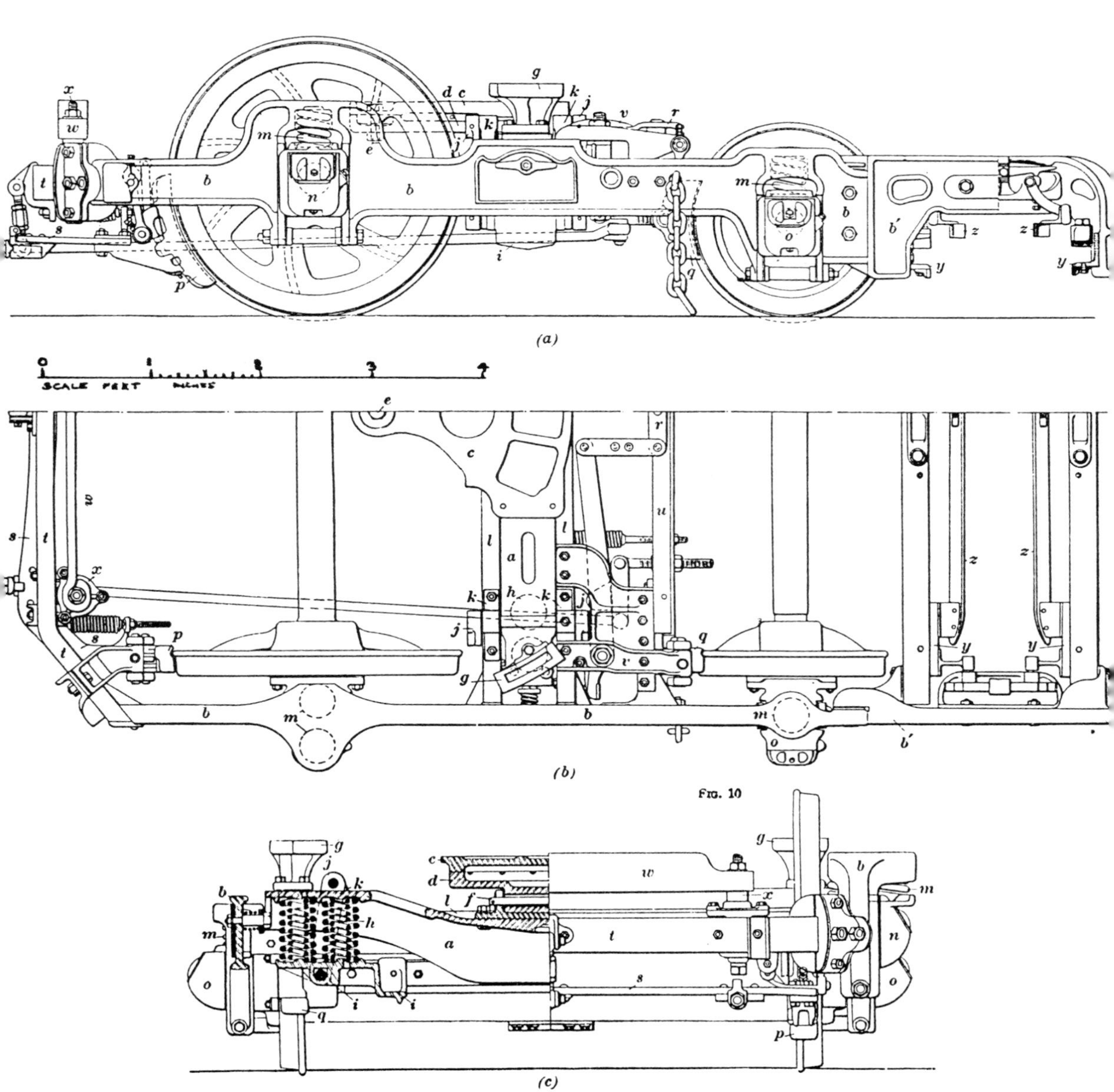

(a)

(b)

(c)

Fig. 10

London County Council Maximum-Traction Truck.—In Fig. 10 is shown a centre-bearing swing-bolster maximum-traction truck, which is specially fitted with a plough carrier, for use on the conduit system of the London County Council Tramways. The side elevation, plan, and half-sectional elevation are shown, respectively, in views (*a*), (*b*), and (*c*). The bolster a is a hollow casting that extends nearly the full width of the truck between the side bars b. The car body rests on the top quadrant or swivel plate c, which is pivoted to the lower swivel plate d at the pivotal point e. The lower plate d, in turn, is hinged to the bolster at f, so that the swivel plates may rock slightly, if necessary, to equalize the distribution of the load on them. An additional rubbing plate or side cushion g is bolted to each end of the bolster to balance the car body. The nests of helical springs h under each end of the bolster rest on spring planks i, which are in turn hung by links j to brackets k on the transoms l. The whole weight of the car is thus transmitted through the springs h to the transoms l, which are rigidly bolted to the side bars b of the truck frame. The side bars are themselves spring-borne by the helical springs m on the top of the axle boxes n, o.

The brake blocks p, q are applied to the respective wheels by exerting a tension on the brake pull rod, which is not shown, but which is pivoted to the central point of the link r. The driving-wheel brake blocks p are attached to the curved brake beam s, and the blocks and beam are hung from the end sill t of the truck. The pony-wheel brake blocks q are attached to the brake beam u, and are hung from one transom by means of the brackets v. Since there is not room for the motor to be hung between the axles of the truck, the motor support w is carried on the spring pillars x, and these are in turn bolted to the end sill t. Extensions b' of the side bars b of the truck form the side frames of the plough carrier. To allow the truck to swivel freely on curves, and in order that the plough may readily be removed from the car, the runners y, which support the plough, stretch right across the truck, while the electrical contact bars z are 4 feet 5 inches long. The contact bars are curved away toward the ends to provide an entrance for the collector springs with which the plough is fitted. In many cases collector springs are not used, and connection is made to the plough by means of flexible insulated cables.

111. A child's eye view of car 539 allows us a look at some of the platform fittings, and we gain a glimpse into the lower saloon. (D.W.K.Jones)

112. Car 467 was partly reconditioned by London Transport in April 1934. It received repanelled upper deck sides plus recessed destination blind boxes, however, the opportunity was not taken to fit drivers' windscreens. This photo shows the car in September 1937 only a few days before it was withdrawn from service. (D.W.K.Jones)

ADVERTISING ON TRAMCARS

Throughout the tramway era in London, the tramcar was regarded as an ideal "vehicle" for commercial advertising. The companies and municipalties which owned the tramways would derive useful revenue by letting spaces on their tramcars. Indeed, it was often suggested that the annual repaint and revarnish of each member of the fleet could be financed by the advertising dues accrued by that particular car. Whatever the merits of this argument, colourful adverts brightened up the sometimes drab reds and browns featured in many liveries. It should be added that trade messages also appeared printed on the backs of tickets.

113. This South Metropolitan car demonstrates how the traditional British single truck, open top tram was decorated with adverts. Notice the combination of national products - Claymore Whisky, Hudsons Soap - with a purely local message for Rawling's the opticians. Inside the lower saloon product information is displayed on paper strips. Even the step to the platform has its commercial value! (E.G.P.Masterman)

114. The former West Ham bogie cars had a problem, insomuch that the area available for adverts was restricted by narrow spaced mouldings on the top deck sides. A solution seems to have been found here by fixing three enamelled, metal plates together to form CASSENBAUMS. This spacing oddity on these cars did at least save them from the indignity of being plastered with LAST TRAM WEEK posters in July 1952. (J.H.Price Coll.)

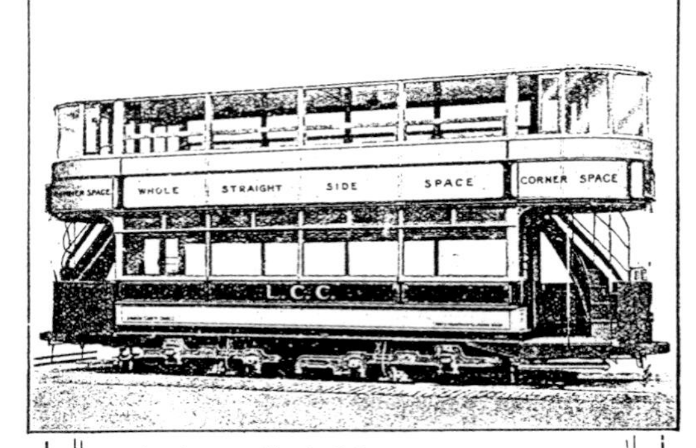

For Information Concerning

ADVERTISING

UPON THE COUNCIL'S

TRAMWAY CARS

Apply to Chief Officer,
London County Council Tramways,
62, Finsbury Pavement, E.C.
Telephone: Nos. 3321, 3322, 3323, London Wall.

←

The LCC used this page in the 1911 Tramways Guide to inform potential advertisers.

→

116. The LCC, as befitted its status, was concerned to make the public aware of new travel facilities. This August 1930 view shows one of the new E3 cars covered with information on cheap fares. (LCC official photo)

115. The author has to admit that he particularly dislikes public transport vehicles which have been "themed" by all over advertising. The nearest London came to this concept was MET car 318 which was painted light blue to promote a sole product - PALMOLIVE SOAP. When this tram was constructed in 1927, the Metropolitan Electric Tramways painters almost went out on strike when "blackleg" sign writers hired by Palmolive arrived at the gates of Hendon Depot! (MET official photo)

IMPROVE
YOUR TRADE
OUTLOOK

BY ADVERTISING
ON WINDOWS
OF TRAMS

TRANSPARENCIES
IN SETS OF THREE

OBLONG 20in. × 6in.
OVAL 9in. × 6in.

ENQUIRIES TO
COMMERCIAL
ADVERTISING
OFFICER
55 BROADWAY
S.W.1. VIC 6880

London Transport was also alive to the possibilities of advertising in the lower saloons of tramcars.

117. Gradually the old enamelled plate adverts were replaced by paper posters. The year's rental for a "wholeside", as seen on car 2239, would be around £16. The following Feltham type car possessed enough space for two "demisides", and each of these came out at around £14 for a twelve month period. (D.W.K.Jones)

FINALE

118. The Aldgate, Minories Trolleybus and Green Line Coach Station was first used in 1939. It was a spacious set up fully in tune with the new image the LPTB wished to project. Ironically, not even this devotion to modernity could move the City Fathers to allow trolleybuses any further into their hallowed territory. Thus the replacing vehicles suffered the same drawbacks as the trams, and passengers still had to change to continue their journey westwards, or they took a motor bus! (C.Carter)

2325 **Conversion to Trolleybus Operation—Route 77**

Notice to Inspectors, Drivers and Conductors.

Commencing on Sunday, September 10th Route 77 will operate as trolleybus route 677, between Smithfield and West India Docks via Goswell Road and Clerkenwell Road.

FARES.

Fares to and from Smithfield will be the same as now apply to and from Aldersgate.

TRANSFERS.

Transfers now available to and from Aldersgate will in future be available to and from Smithfield.

Extract from LT circular, September 1939

119. A less grand arrangement existed at West India Docks terminus. Again a simple tramway single track stub had to be replaced by a turning circle placed in a convenient side street. The 677 trolleybus route lasted from Sunday, 10th September 1939 to Tuesday, 14th April 1959. (C.Carter)

END OF THE LINE

120. A mist drifts up from the Thames and the photographer risks a time exposure shot of this 77 tram with the crew safely ensconced in the lower saloon. Not only would service 77 soon disappear, but the face of the East End would be changed forever by the Second World War. Quiet moments like this would be at a premium in the next few years. (T.M.Russell Coll.)